100 ICONIC

BOLLYWOOD COSTUMES

100 ICONIC BOLLYWOOD COSTUMES

TEXT **SUJATA ASSOMULL**   ILLUSTRATIONS **APARNA RAM**

FOREWORD **MANISH MALHOTRA**

Lustre Press
Roli Books

For each film, the credited costume designer is taken from the film's opening and ending credits. The order and the names (which sometimes include vendor names) are taken directly from the film. This template has been consistently followed except with films where no credit has been given. In these cases, both the writer and publisher made every effort to research to whom the credit ought to be given. This was the process throughout the book, as it seemed the most decisive method to gain the correct data.

© **ROLI BOOKS 2019**

Published in India by Roli Books

M-75, Greater Kailash II Market, New Delhi -110 048, India

Ph: ++91-11-4068 2000, E-mail: info@rolibooks.com

Website: www.rolibooks.com

ISBN: 978-81-941109-7-2

Editor: Saachi Khurana
Design: Sneha Pamneja
Layout: Naresh L. Mondal
Pre-press: Jyoti Dey

Printed in India

CONTENTS

FOREWORD

Manish Malhotra

I generally believe that films have always influenced fashion in India. Take the 1960s and *Mughal-e-Azam*, or the 1970s and *Pakeezah* – their style is iconic. People have always looked to movies for style inspiration. Think of Sharmila Tagore's sleeveless knotted blouses with her bouffant hair and chiffon saris, and of Rajesh Khanna's guru collar and kurta shirts. The list is endless. Let's also not forget how the storytelling of iconic filmmakers, from Guru Dutt to Karan Johar, have influenced style. What fascinates me is how filmmakers have worked with costume designers to create these beautiful looks. From *Aan* to *Mughal-e-Azam* to *Pakeezah* to *Bobby* to *Chandni*, style was embedded in all aspects of the film, from the music to the clothes. When these elements work together, that then is real magic.

I practically grew up in movie theatres and was wide-eyed about cinema and its use of colours. It pushed me into pursuing drawing and art classes and led to me becoming a costume designer in the 1990s, a time when style had gone out of movies. My idea was to have fashion meet film again by mixing styling with costumes. Before that, there were fabulous costume designers like Bhanu Athaiya, but costumes were not considered a part of the visual look of a film and treated very 'separately', I feel. For instance, today a bridal look is not just about the outfit, but about the make-up, hair, jewellery and setting. The first film I worked on was *Swarg* with Juhi Chawla in the 1990s. I went on to do *Gumrah* with Sridevi, and after this I never looked back. In February 2019, I completed 29 years of costume styling. It reflects my struggles, resilience, hard work, passion and love for clothes and films; repeatedly connecting with the youth, and continuously being relevant with changing times.

The early 1990s was a phase when young Non-Resident Indians (NRIs) were searching for a new take on Indian fashion. Having not grown up in India like their parents, they were looking for something that was modern and had an international feel, and yet respected the traditions that their parents expected when it came to dressing 'Indian'. There was a gap that needed to be filled and in many ways it was the fashion of films that gave NRIs what they were looking for, like the asymmetrical top over the *sharara* that Kareena Kapoor wore in *Kabhi Khushi Kabhie Gham*. That, in many ways, was the look that led to today's modern lehenga.

It is now passé when fashion insiders feel that film is not a part of their world. Who decides this fact? Today every designer in the country gives clothes to actors to wear. Of course, not every film will display a lot of fashion, because it may not suit the characters. But you can be inspired by a colour or cut you see in a film. As the film industry becomes bigger and we see more types of films being made, we see more types of fashion on screen. From costume dramas to period films to biopics, the emphasis is on an authentic look. It is a good time to be a part of the industry; there is a lovely change and so much variety, with social media amplifying the relationship between everything, especially film and fashion.

This is why there is a need for a book that highlights the fact that films have always been influential where fashion and style are concerned. For example, in *Jab We Met*, that T-shirt and salwar that Kareena Kapoor wore as Geet became a big phenomenon, and it is now a way of life, with many young women wearing a salwar with a T-shirt or a denim jacket with a kurta. Just as Geet's character was approachable and lively, so were her clothes.

I am delighted that there is a book documenting iconic and influential looks in films. I congratulate and wish Sujata Assomull and Aparna Ram all the best for taking us on this journey of fashion in film and honouring the work, talent and hardships that have gone into making these films. It is about time that film's influence on Indian fashion is acknowledged.

INTRODUCTION

Sujata Assomull

When two forms of art, one visual and the other applied, come together, they create a seamless moment that is remembered forever. This is how film and fashion complement each other. How can we forget the polka-dot, cropped blouse that Dimple Kapadia flaunted so effortlessly in *Bobby*, or the Hermès Kelly, a.k.a. Bagwati, that was almost a character in itself in *Zindagi Na Milegi Dobara*?

What began as a book of fashion illustrations from Hindi cinema with London-based Aparna Ram (a former investment banker turned illustrator) transformed into a nostalgic journey through the most iconic fashion moments of Indian cinema. With illustration, fashion's oldest form of visual documentation, presently going through a renaissance, it is the perfect medium to take one through some of the most stylish looks worn by women in the Hindi film industry (or Bollywood, as it is fondly called). We hope to show how clothes, as costumes, play an integral role in cinematic language and how fashion, when crafted well, can help flesh out a film character and give birth to wider trends. Nowhere is this more apparent than in Bollywood. We decided to start with *Aan* (1952), India's first Technicolor film, and to close with *Veere Di Wedding* (2018), a film wherein fashion almost serves as one of the lead characters.

Fashion, as seen in films, tells a story in a similar way fashion on the catwalk does. It interacts with the aesthetics and norms of the times: Sharmila Tagore wearing a blue printed swimsuit in *An Evening in Paris* in 1967 was considered so risqué that India's public television station, Doordarshan, edited the song out; barely five years later, Nutan, Zeenat Aman and Dimple Kapadia wearing swimsuits did not create much of a sensation. More recently, when Alia Bhatt wore a yellow bikini in her debut film, *Student of the Year*, it was considered completely normal. But films in India reach an audience no runway or fashion magazine could dream of. That is how Kareena Kapoor's Patiala salwars worn with T-shirts in *Jab We Met* and Deepika Padukone's knotted off-shoulder T-shirts in *Cocktail* became every college girl's must-have. Think of the short and bright collared kurtas worn in *Bunty Aur Babli*, or the 'glamazon' vibe

Polka Play: This crop top worn by Dimple Kapadia in her debut film, *Bobby* (1973), spoke of a carefree innocence so iconic that films continue to refer to it.

exuded by Rekha in *Khoon Bhari Maang* that compelled many women to change the way they dressed. These looks went from the screen to the street instantly – even red carpet looks do not command such an instant appeal. When London's Victoria and Albert Museum held an exhibition called 'The Fabric of India' in 2015, among the selected pieces was a mirror-work ghagra that Abu Jani–Sandeep Khosla created for the publicity stills of Sanjay Leela Bhansali's *Devdas*. Worn by Madhuri Dixit, it had real zardozi work and weighed 10 kilograms; while it may not have featured in the actual film, the impressive ensemble was given a place of pride at the show.

Neeta Lulla, a seasoned costume designer, has worked on projects ranging from the above mentioned *Devdas* to Ashutosh Gowariker's *Jodhaa Akbar*, the latter of which can be credited for reminding the youth of the beauty of uncut and *polki* jewellery. The jewellery brand Tanishq even tied up with the filmmakers to create a special collaborative collection. The movie also successfully revived a textile type popular during Mughal times: the Mughals were known to enjoy Dhakai cottons, and to recreate this look, Neeta Lulla turned to mulmul cottons – something that Indian contemporary fashion associated only with day dressing. The mulmul costumes were embellished through traditional techniques such as *resham* and truly uplifted the national outlook on cotton. That year, mulmul become de rigueur in many fashion boutiques' festive collections.

It was in 1994 that I started my career as a journalist, working at a Mumbai-based business magazine. My editor then had asked me if I had watched *Hum Aapke Hain Koun..!* Back in 1994, the film's stupendous success was the talk of the town. Given that I had just moved from the United Kingdom, my Hindi was still not up to speed – although I did often queue outside London's Odeon Marble Arch on the evenings they showed the occasional Hindi film. My editor insisted that I watch the movie: if our readers had liked it, then I, as a lifestyle writer, needed to truly understand what aspects of the film were influential and appealing to them. Ultimately, this Sooraj Barjatya film felt like an extended wedding video to me, but I could not deny how integral fashion was to it; like everyone else, I simply had to own the purple sari that Madhuri Dixit wore in the song '*Didi Tera Devar Deewana*'. On my next trip to London, I rushed to Southall to buy a plain purple charmeuse sari, and once I returned to India, I sourced some gold borders and designed my own version of that iconic look.

That is pretty much how it worked during the 1990s. There were no fashion weeks in India. If you didn't pick up on trends while flipping through the pages of women's lifestyle magazines (there were also no real fashion titles at the time), you would turn to films and film stars for inspiration. Fourteen years later, when I became the launch editor

The Original 'Kira Kira' Outfit: This hand-embroidered lehenga was so heavy it was used only for the posters of Sanjay Leela Bhansali's *Devdas* (2002), and not the film itself. Yet it was so memorable that it was later part of an exhibit at London's Victoria and Albert Museum.

of *Harper's Bazaar India*, my knowledge of Indian cinema was to deepen – our cover girls were nearly always actresses. Fashion purists have often criticized this, but the fact is that in India, for many women, film remains an inspiration.

There was a time when wearing or designing 'filmi' fashion was frowned upon. This has changed today, in part due to the advent of multiplexes. The first multiplex opened in Delhi in June 1997, and today's industry reports estimate that 60 per cent of the film industry's revenue come from multi-screen cinemas. This has also helped independent filmmakers gain a platform, and their more 'real' and sometimes more urban and slick takes on cinema have found resonance with middle-class audiences in India.

As the industry has grown more profitable, it has also become more professional. From simply requiring various 'dress men', wives of filmmakers and actors themselves to work on a movie's costumes, to employing dedicated costume designers to create a look, there has been an enormous change in the way cinema has incorporated fashion. Rocky S. is a designer who has worked on more than 200 films, including *Mohra* (for the yellow sari with frill sleeves that rain-soaked Raveena Tandon wore in '*Tip Tip Barsa Paani*') and *Corporate* (for the pinstriped, business look of Bipasha Basu). He recalls that, when he first started out as a costume designer, he would receive a call from the director to make an ensemble overnight. There was little planning and no real budget, and he would often have to haggle over payment after the shooting was finished. Today there is a separate fund allocated for costumes. For example, at the time of this writing, there is a big-budget production of around Rs. 250 crores that Rocky is working on; he estimates that about 3 per cent of the total is now reserved solely for costumes. (A 2016 report, 'Indywood, The Indian Film Industry', by Deloitte noted that the average cost of a Hindi film is Rs. 15 crores).

Sensing the growing importance of fashion, the Filmfare Awards – one of India's leading awards for cinema – instituted the category 'Best Costume Designer' in 1995. The first recipient of the award was Manish Malhotra for his work in Ram Gopal Varma's *Rangeela*. With his reel and runway experience, Manish Malhotra is easily one of India's most influential voices in fashion. Having worked in the industry for almost 30 years, his formidable list includes *Judaai*, *Rangeela*, *Kabhi Khushi Kabhie Gham...*, *Student of the Year* and *Mom*. He started his label in 2005, and many of his iconic film costumes, such as Deepika Padukone's frill sari in *Yeh Jawaani Hai Deewani* and Preity

Reel Over Ramp: Many fashion trends today have exploded due to their 'filmi' origins and have a far greater impact than what you see on the ramps of any of the Indian fashion weeks.

 11

Zinta's nude lehenga in *Kal Ho Naa Ho*, have become evergreens – and he still receives orders from private clients based on these designs.

Today, be it a home-grown designer or an international brand, the priority is no doubt to dress an actor for the big screen rather than to do so for a red-carpet event or a magazine cover (even if it is *Vogue* or *Harper's Bazaar*). Such is the allure of cinema. According to 'Indywood, The Indian Film Industry', Indian cinema is the largest in terms of films produced, with 1,500–2,000 films made in a year; Hindi films are the largest player. India has the second-highest footfall at cinemas globally, second only to China (the report states that 2.1 billion Indians went to the cinema in 2015). This means that if you want to reach the upper classes or the masses, film is probably your best bet, provided you find the right project. Many international luxury brands have therefore worked closely with new-age filmmakers such as Karan Johar and Rhea Kapoor; indeed, Louis Vuitton and Christian Dior can thank Karan Johar's *Kabhi Alvida Naa Kehna* for alerting Indians about their arrival in the country. Leading Indian fashion designers such as Anju Modi, Sabyasachi Mukherjee, Abu Jani and Sandeep Khosla have all crossed over to work in films as costume designers.

Today we talk about films joining the Rs. 1,000 crore club since it is no longer considered consequential for a successful commercial Hindi movie to have global box-office revenues in excess of even Rs. 100 crore. But with clothing in India being such an unorganised sector, you could probably count fashion designers who make more than Rs. 100 crore on two hands. Needless to say, in India, there is no bigger or better marketing tool for designers than films.

For young designers like Swapnil Shinde, the winner of reality television show *Lakmé Fashion House*, it is film that works as a catalyst to ensure success. Swapnil has worked on clothes for movies like *Fashion* and *Bang Bang*; he is not a costume designer, but the fact that his label is associated with Indian film is enough. The white gown with the side cut-out and black details that Katrina Kaif wore in *Bang Bang* is something his studio still makes today on special request. Luxury holiday label Shivan and Narresh, whose fashion week's presentations are considered a hot ticket, created vintage-inspired swimwear for Anushka Sharma in Anurag Kashyap's *Bombay Velvet*. The design aesthetic was created with the jazz era of the Maximum City in mind and used woven fabrics on high-waisted bralette bikinis. It was a high-profile movie and the actress was an influential one, so for a young brand it was a strong communication tool and helped drive sales. Similarly, niche high-end jewellery brand Sunita Shekhawat's uncut diamond earrings featuring enamel work, and *maang tika* with uncut diamonds and South Sea pearls, were worn by Sonam Kapoor in *Veere Di Wedding*. While this bespoke jeweller

The Film & Fashion Love/Hate Affair: Many of India's leading couturiers such as Sabyasachi, Abu Jani–Sandeep Khosla and Anju Modi have worked on film costumes, helping to turn them into the household names they are today.

does not duplicate the piece for clients, the label has received new queries from brides-to-be. Such partnerships with film also give brands a social media-friendly image. In this digital age, that picture is truly worth more than a thousand words. An image from a film tends to have a longer sell-by date. Referring to iconic outfits in the right film, such as the anarkalis worn by Rekha in *Umrao Jaan* or the white jumpsuit worn by Zeenat Aman in *Yaadon Ki Baaraat*, never goes out of fashion.

How and why has fashion become so central to Bollywood? Clothing can help define a character and add to his or her personality, even if it is through a detail you may not even immediately notice. When the legendary Bhanu Athaiya added a scarf to many of Mumtaz's ensembles in *Aadmi Aur Insaan*, it gave the actress a prop with which to exude the aura of a femme fatale. Another iconic look that is a product of the Bhanu Athaiya–Mumtaz collaboration is the flaming orange sari of *Brahmachari*. Moulded around Mumtaz's body, it wouldn't be incorrect to say that it was the predecessor to the 'concept sari', now a staple in every couturier's collection. The way that sari was made gave Mumtaz the freedom to move effortlessly in the song 'Aajkal Tere Mere Pyaar Ke Charche'. For some directors, fashion has become an intrinsic part of their work – for instance, Raj Kapoor and the wet saris in *Satyam Shivam Sundaram* and *Ram Teri Ganga Maili*, or Yash Chopra and the white kameezes in *Chandni* and *Dil To Pagal Hai*. You can see today's young filmmakers refer to this phenomenon in their films – Karan Johar's penchant for chiffon saris can be seen as an ode to Yash Chopra, a man he calls his mentor. And in turn, producer Rhea Kapoor's use of international brands in *Aisha* and *Veere Di Wedding* takes forward a trend started by Karan Johar.

There is ultimately no question that films impact the way many Indian women dress, and this is what we raise a toast to in *100 Iconic Bollywood Costumes*. In picking out some of fashion's most iconic moments in film, this book traces the cultural history of both cinema and costume design in India, and will be of interest to fashion students, art historians and anyone who enjoys Bollywood. Though we did begin this project by also including men and red carpet looks, we soon realized that we were covering far too wide of a scope. Perhaps this book will spin off its own sequels.

As part of our research, we spoke to a number of professionals in the industry, including editors, critics and directors, to add expert commentary on the films we looked at. The films chosen are ones that everyone involved had a strong recall for, had on-screen looks that inspired trends or were later copied in other movies. While this is not a definitive list, it represents how Indian fashion has changed through the years, how it always reflects the aesthetics of the time and how it impacts everyday style.

On-Screen Statements: From a *maang tika* on the forehead, to slippers on the feet – the right accessory worn at the right moment by the right actress in a film can quickly become a season's must-have.

1950s & 1960s

1952
Nadira

Aan

Credited Costume Designers
Fazal Din, Chagan Jivan and Alla Ditta

In 1952, Mehboob Khan's *Aan* was, domestically, India's highest grossing film – and it was also the country's first picture to be filmed in full Technicolor. Costumes had never looked so vibrant. The film is about a royal love story, and its costumes were appropriately lavish, influenced by Hollywood films of that era. It starred the famous Dilip Kumar, Prem Nath and Nimmi, was released as *The Savage Princess* in the UK and US and played in cinemas around the world. Although critics found the performances wooden, Nadira (as Princess Rajshree) stole the show, mostly thanks to her look.

Aan marked the debut of Nadira. Her full name was Florence Ezekiel Nadira and she hailed from a Baghdadi Jewish family; it was her 'Western'-looking features that bagged her this role. It was rumoured that both Madhubala and Nargis were considered for the part but Nadira won out, as Khan wanted the film to have 'international appeal'. She soon brought a new look to Hindi films as she was happy to wear skimpy sari blouses and strapless gowns – what may seem conservative today was considered controversial back then. In *Aan*, however, she introduced a sense of androgyny to Indian cinema. Playing a feisty, horse-loving princess, she wore fitted jackets with exaggerated shoulders, cravat-style scarves and high-waisted jodhpurs, bringing a new take on sensual dressing. Her hair and make-up seems inspired by the legendary actress of Hollywood's Golden Age, Marlene Dietrich.

A few years before Nadira passed away in 2006, I interviewed her for a leading Indian daily. By this time she was living alone in her South Mumbai apartment, and said that one of her proudest achievements was maintaining a less than 21-inch waist during her heyday. *Aan's* high-waisted jodhpurs clearly showed off this figure. And since these were pre-costume designer days, Nadira also explained, she was very involved in all her looks. Even as a newcomer she understood the importance of costume, hair and make-up in a movie.

Aan remains a seminal film even today. It introduced Nadira as Indian film's ultimate seducer and one of its original vamps: Bollywood's version of femme fatales.

1960
Madhubala

Mughal-e-Azam

Credited Costume Designer
B.N. Trivedi (wardrobe in-charge)

This is a film that will always be considered one of Indian cinema's finest. Madhubala played Anarkali, a role based on the legendary Mughal courtesan from the court of Akbar. Prince Salim (Dilip Kumar), the son of Emperor Akbar (Prithviraj Kapoor), falls in love and hopes to marry her. However, she is imprisoned by the emperor, who disapproves of the relationship. *Mughal-e-Azam* broke all box-office records at the time, and gained a new generation of fans in 2004 when it became the first black-and-white Hindi film to be digitally coloured. And in the colour version, the beauty of the costumes truly comes to life.

While there was a dedicated costume department that worked on the film, the fashion was really about the director's vision. Director K. Asif wanted everything to be as authentic as possible, from the grand sets to the beautiful jewellery, which was all real. Footwear was ordered from Agra, crowns were made by the skilled craftsmen of Kolhapur and much of the jewellery came from the city known for its goldsmiths, Hyderabad. Fabrics were rich, with silk brocades embroidered with real zari, and colours were regal and vibrant. The most expensive film of that era, no money was spared on any details, and in her book titled *I, Durga Khote: An Autobiography*, the actress who plays Salim's mother, Jodhabai, recalls how lavish the costumes of this film were. This was a big-budget film, reportedly costing Rs. 1.5 crores back then. Indian cinema had rarely seen something this grand.

In the film's most famous song, '*Pyaar Kiya To Darna Kya*', Anarkali wears a style of dress that is popular with Kathak dancers – a high-waisted kameez with a full skirt. In striking red and light blue, the look is completed with a Mughal-style cap and lots of jewellery. The famous silhouette is known as the anarkali, after the renowned courtesan herself. You can therefore credit this film for reviving both the myth of Anarkali the courtesan, as well as the iconic kurta shape named after her. It is a true example of how, for fashion in India, there is no better catwalk than the silver screen. Sadly, this film turned out to be Madhubala's last due to her untimely death. Thanks to this film, however, she will always remain a beloved movie star and fashion icon.

1964
Vyjayanthimala

Sangam

Credited Costume Designers
**Vishnu Vellar, Dada Khalikar, Bhanu Athaiya and
Laffans (India) Ltd. (for Vyjayanthimala)**

This was Raj Kapoor's first production in colour and was shot in various locations, including Venice, Paris and Switzerland. Featuring a love triangle between Sunder Khanna (Raj Kapoor), Gopal Verma (Rajendra Kumar) and Radha Khanna (Vyjayanthimala), this was a landmark film for the actress. Although she had taken a break before this film, she came back to play a new-age Indian woman who wore a swimsuit and a sari with equal ease.

It was her white-and-red Bengali-style sari for the song 'Yeh Mera Prem Patra' that stood out, mainly for its simplicity. Teamed with a white blouse, the sari was not pinned to Vyjayanthimala's shoulder, so the *pallu* often gently slipped down to reveal her bare arms, adding just a hint of sensuality. There was emphasis on Vyjayanthimala's expressive kohl-rimmed eyes with plenty of close-ups around her face.

Her costumes were designed by the legendary Bhanu Athaiya. In her book, *The Art of Costume Design*, Bhanu says, 'Raj Saab [Raj Kapoor] gave me an idea of the character Vyjayanthimala was to play. She was to be a modern, educated and spirited young girl, born and brought up in the city. My brief was to make her look elegant, which I achieved by mostly dressing her in white.' Shot against a lush green landscape, the white-and-red sari really stood out, and it was complemented by the red of Vyjayanthimala's nails, bangles and bindi. It was simple yet striking.

1965
Waheeda Rehman

Guide

Credited Costume Designer
Bhanu Athaiya (for Waheeda Rehman)

Based on the novel *The Guide* by R.K. Narayan, *Guide* was directed by Vijay Anand and had Dev Anand playing Raju, a former convict and a tourist guide, and Waheeda Rehman playing Rosie, the neglected wife of an ageing archaeologist. Rosie is the daughter of a courtesan, who gained respectability through her marriage; but this meant that she had to turn her back on her passion – dancing. As the film progresses, Raju 'guides' and encourages her to once again become a dancer. *Guide* was India's official submission to the Oscars for Best Foreign Film that year.

The costumes for Waheeda were designed by Bhanu Athaiya. For a large part of the film, Waheeda wore beautiful drapes with modest blouses that were teamed with silver jewellery; she also wore a *parandi* in her hair. She became the epitome of elegance at that time. Says Nonita Kalra, editor of *Harper's Bazaar India*, 'Clothing is simply something on a hanger until the wearer transforms it. And that is why actors are often at the forefront of style – they make clothing or an outfit into an entity, a being, by bringing individuality to it. Ms. Rehman wore her saris, her *parandis*, her jewellery with a simplicity that sometimes belied the layering.'

As Rosie transforms into a dancer, her style changes. For the song 'Saiyaan Beimaan', she wears a costume that is all about dance. It is a classical Amrapali costume and has touches of a Bharatanatyam dancer's outfit. The blouse at first looks like a bandeau, but, deceptively, it is a blouse with a skin-coloured high neck and elbow-length sleeves; this is because Waheeda was uncomfortable baring her arms. In *The Art of Costume Design*, Bhanu says, 'As the film progressed, Rosie transformed from a regular city girl to a professional classical dancer.' In this film, you see how Bhanu was able to make costumes become a seamless part of the cinematic narrative.

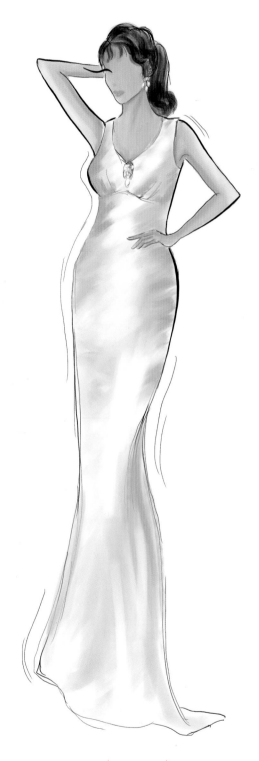

1965
Nanda

Jab Jab Phool Khile

Credited Costume Designers
Narendra Kumar and Amber's Gowns (for Nanda)

Although Nanda had already been in the film industry for more than 15 years when the movie was released, *Jab Jab Phool Khile* marked a landmark moment in her career. In this romantic drama, she played the role of Rita, opposite Shashi Kapoor as Raja. Nanda and Shashi went on to do many films together, but for Nanda, this role was particularly important as this was the first project in which she played a glamour girl.

A child star, she was known as Baby Nanda in the late 1940s and 1950s, before progressing to become a leading lady. This film proved that she could play a range of roles, from the devoted wife of an army major in *Hum Dono* (1961) to the Westernized and fashionable heiress that her character, Rita, embodies in this movie. Shashi's character is far humbler by comparison; he is the owner of a houseboat in Kashmir. When Rita goes to Kashmir on holiday, she meets him and a romance starts, but given their difference in social backgrounds, and since Rita has already been promised by her father to another man, the course of love does not run smooth.

The opening credits have a special mention: 'Miss Nanda's Costumes: Amber Gowns'. It was common, at the time, for upmarket retail stores in Bombay to work closely with films to supply them with a wardrobe, particularly when it came to sourcing Western ensembles. This is clear right from the opening scene, where Rita wears a white knee-length pencil skirt with a matching cardigan and a blue top. She carries a large straw tote bag with dark sunglasses and a white scarf draped over her head, and her hair is worn short in an in-and-out turn style. You can tell that the character of Rita is one that was in tune with the latest trends in Europe.

In the song, *'Ye Samaa Samaa Hai Pyaar Ka'*, Rita is seen openly wooing Raja in a lingerie-style, off-white satin dress, with winged eyeliner and coral lips, and a brooch strategically placed in the middle of her deep 'V' neckline. This was probably Nanda's most alluring moment on screen, with all her curves on display.

1965
Sadhana

Waqt

Credited Costume Designer
Bhanu Athaiya

A family-based drama that was also a romance, this film, directed by Yash Chopra, had a star-studded cast. It tells the story of three sons of a prosperous merchant who have an idyllic life until an earthquake changes everything, and the boys end up being separated. Raja (Raaj Kumar) is raised by a criminal and turns into a suave thief. The second son, Ravi (Sunil Dutt), is adopted by a rich couple. Vijay (Shashi Kapoor) remains in Delhi to look after the mother. The glam quotient is brought in by the two female leads: Sharmila Tagore as the rich college girl, Renu, who falls in love with Vijay, along with Sadhana as Meena, the love interest of Raja.

While there is no question that Sharmila, known for her personal style, looked sensational in this film, it was Sadhana who became the fashion star of the movie. Since *Waqt* was mainly about people from privileged families, the women's costumes reflected how fashion was used as a status symbol in India by the upper classes. It also experimented with its fashion choices. The salwar kameez was starting to grow in popularity in movies as the college girl's choice of clothing. In *Waqt*, this loose salwar was traded in for the tighter churidar, whilst the kameez boasted a tight cut and was above the knee in length – almost like a form-fitting dress. Sadhana teamed this modern take on a traditional Indian silhouette with her Audrey Hepburn-inspired hair – what became known as the 'Sadhana fringe'. The kameez-churidar went on to become the uniform for unmarried women on and off screen.

It is not surprising that the person behind this look is the legendary Bhanu Athaiya, who is considered to be India's first real costume designer – she later went on to become the first Indian to win an Oscar for her work in Richard Attenborough's *Gandhi*. Says Bhanu Athaiya in her book, *The Art of Costume Design*, 'In *Waqt* we introduced the churidar pyjamas and sleeveless fitted kurtas with a side band that brought complete attention to the body form.' Bhanu goes on to say that *Waqt* 'ushered a revolution in the fashion scene in India.' The Lycra-legging-style churidar, which you now find in department stores such as Westside and Lifestyle, can be traced back to this look.

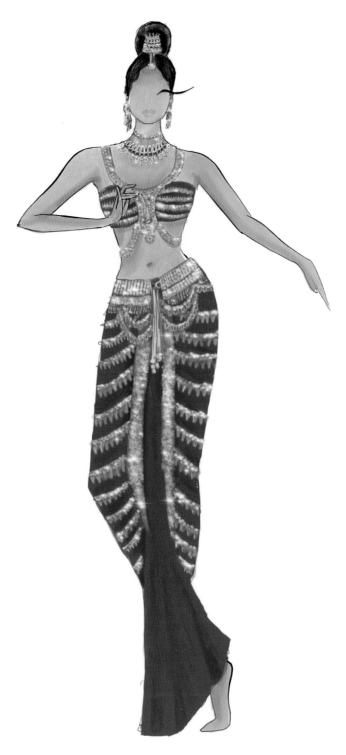

1966

Vyjayanthimala

Amrapali

Credited Costume Designer
Bhanu Athaiya

A historical film set in the fourth century, *Amrapali* is based on the love story between the court dancer, Amrapali, and the king of Magadh, Ajatashatru, with Vyjayanthimala and Sunil Dutt playing the lead characters. Historically, Amrapali was no ordinary court dancer – her beauty and grace inspired poets, writers and artisans of that time. She later became a disciple of Gautam Buddha. In the movie, as the court's most talented dancer, she is dressed in a way that represents both her poise and her sensuality.

The 'Amrapali sari', as it is now known, is a dhoti drape worn with a bustier. In the film it is adorned with a generous dose of gold ornamental jewellery. Bhanu Athaiya, the costume designer behind this look, travelled to the Ajanta caves to study the frescoes of that time in order to incoporate them into her designs (the *mahurat* of the film was held at these caves too). The most remembered Amrapali outfit is in a distinct shade of orange – a colour that, in the Buddhist era, came from a dye made from *parijat* flowers and was the chosen hue of monks' robes.

This Amrapali style has been revisited multiple times in other Indian films such as *Asoka* (2001), in which Kareena Kapoor wore a Manish Malhotra drape, and *Himmatwala* (1983), where Sridevi was seen in a similar costume. You can sense a reference to the work of nineteenth-century painter Raja Ravi Varma in all these outfits. Indeed, Bhanu says that, for her, this assignment was a 'dream come true' as she always had a passion for classical Indian art forms.

1966

Helen

Teesri Manzil

Credited Costume Designers
Mrs. Parekh, Bhanu Athaiya, Leena Shah and Bilquis Khan

Directed by Vijay Anand, this crime thriller was one of the most important movies of the 1960s. Rocky (Shammi Kapoor), the heart-throb drummer of a band, is accused of breaking the heart of Sunita's (Asha Parekh) elder sister, who was so shaken by Rocky's snub that she apparently committed suicide. Sunita wants Rocky to pay for his role in her sister's death. Then there is Ruby (Helen), a dancer in the club Rocky performs in, who is in love with him. This is a 'whodunnit' thriller that has you guessing who the killer is till the very end.

It is the cabaret costumes of the original 'item girl', Helen, that have had the most visual impact on the industry, especially in the song, '*O Haseena Zulfonwali Jaane Jahan*'. The song opens with a play of shadows and a through-the-looking-glass feel to add to its fantastical style. In true Bollywood fashion, Helen goes through a range of costume and wig changes during this one song. This includes a Spanish-style flamenco dress in red, with black lace details and an oversized flower worn on the crown of her head. The silhouette was fitted around Helen's waistline in order to show off her figure. She was known to enjoy playing dress-up for her films but also deeply understood the importance of costume to the overall story. This song is an ode to that.

The set for this number can only be described as brash, yet your eyes are firmly fixed on Helen, who truly was the ultimate showgirl. Bhanu Athaiya says of the flamenco-style dress, 'I have created many Western cabaret costumes for Helen; however, this Spanish costume from the song "*O Haseena Zulfonwali*" is my favourite.'

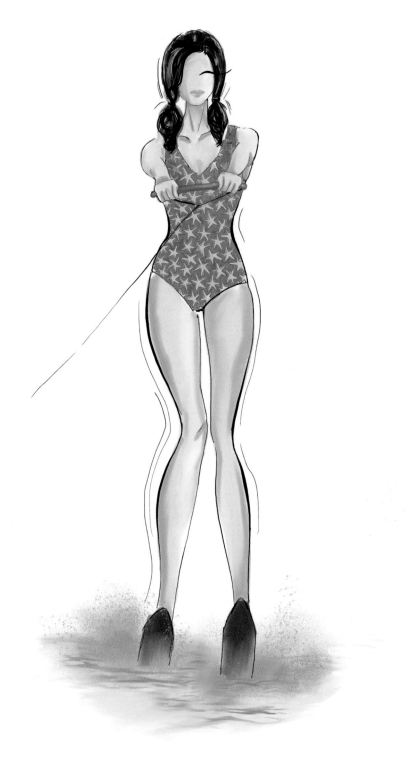

1967
Sharmila Tagore

An Evening in Paris

Credited Costume Designers
Vasant Chauhan, Mani Rabadi and Miss Johar

This stylish 1960s film was shot in Paris, Beirut, Niagara Falls and Switzerland, and was a visual delight. Sharmila Tagore had a double role as Deepa, a rich Indian woman who goes to Paris looking for love and finds it in the arms of Sam (Shammi Kapoor), and as Suzy, a club dancer. As one would expect from any Bollywood movie, the plot thickens when a gangster abducts Deepa. Working closely on the looks of this film was Mani Rabadi, who was known to enjoy making her female protagonists glamorous.

Sharmila's role demanded skin and sensuality and, as a non-conformist, she was more than happy to wear a bikini for the movie. The director, Shakti Samanta, felt it was too risqué, however, and didn't want unnecessary scandal: indeed, shot in 1967, this film came out at a time when India's film censorship board was debating if even kissing should be allowed on screen. So Sharmila wore a blue one-piece as she skimmed the water on jet skis, whilst Shammi Kapoor serenaded her from a helicopter with the song 'Aasman Se Aaya Farishta'.

Interestingly, when you mention An Evening in Paris, many will mistakenly say this was the first Indian film in which an actress wore a two-piece swimsuit on screen. With her low pigtails, black eyeliner and hourglass figure, Sharmila caused a stir without actually wearing a bikini. Indian public television station Doordarshan aired the film minus the demure one-piece, as they considered even that too revealing. But Sharmila did get to wear her bikini soon after, for a shoot for Filmfare magazine at the time of the film's promotion.

It was this movie that changed Indian cinema's approach to dressing when it came to swimwear. Suddenly it was acceptable for the leading actress to be dressed in swimwear if it was appropriate for the scene; showing skin was no longer reserved for the vamps.

1967
Helen

Jewel Thief

Credited Costume Designer
Mani Rabadi

A spy thriller by Vijay Anand, known to be inspired by Alfred Hitchcock, this film was obviously an ode to James Bond. In the lead was Vijay's dapper brother Dev Anand in a double role as Vinay and Prince Amar. There were also four Bond-style femme fatales in the film, including Anju Mahendru, Tanuja, Faryal and Helen, the vamp.

Helen's cabaret number from *Jewel Thief* is considered one of her most iconic and memorable, and her costume played a big part in shaping this legacy. In the song *'Baithe Hain Kya Uske Paas'*, she wore a red-sequined, leotard-styled costume featuring animal-print details on the bust, with black and white ostrich plumes attached to the back of the outfit. It was finished with sheer sparkling stockings and a tiara in her beehive hair. Even her heeled shoes were encrusted with crystals. While at first glance her dress looked like a bustier, it was in fact a sleeveless outfit, and as the camera moved closely onto Helen, you clearly saw a nude covering on the shoulders that had more sparkles encrusted in it; Helen was known to wear body stockings under most of her outfits to maintain modesty. She never looked vulgar, no matter how skimpy her outfit was. *'Baithe Hain Kya Uske Paas'* was meant to be an over-the-top bar dance number that seductively stood out in this slick movie. Says Priya Tanna, editor of *Vogue India*, 'We don't credit Helen enough for her contribution to fashion and film. The way she showed skin in a very sexy and classy way is something we can take cues from even today. She brought body confidence to Bollywood [and] was India's first siren.'

The film marked the beginning of a long-standing relationship between Helen and costume designer Mani Rabadi. The exotic costume Rabadi crafted was carried with élan by Helen, or 'H-Bomb', as she was also known, and it was a match that worked well. In the song, she oozed both sensuality and poise. Her look may seem over the top today, perhaps even bordering on outrageous, but many modern item girls are inspired by her – be it Malaika Arora or Kareena Kapoor. To be an item girl, you have to stand out and be both bold and beautiful, and Helen knew this very well.

1967
Vyjayanthimala

Jewel Thief

Credited Costume Designer
Mani Rabadi

The leading lady of the film was Vyjayanthimala as Shalini, a woman who would have everyone believe she is engaged to Amar. The role had originally been written for Saira Banu, who was considered one of the film industry's most stylish heroines at that time. But she opted out after her marriage to Dilip Kumar, and so the woman known for her poise, Vyjayanthimala, stepped in.

Mani Rabadi worked on this film as the costume designer and created some very fashionable looks for all its female characters. For Vyjayanthimala, she stuck to beautiful drapes, and one specific sari became a real conversation point. It was a red sari with a 3D-style appliqué of white fluffy balls, resembling polka dots, and many people called it the 'cotton-ball sari'. She wore this in the song 'Dil Pukare Aare Aare'. It was finished with a mustard-coloured coat, drop earrings, a chic updo and winged eyeliner on those expressive eyes. Mani Rabadi liked the use of polka dots on screen; she would later dress Dimple Kapadia in a cropped polka-dot tie-front shirt in Bobby.

But with a coat over that cotton ball design, Vyjayanthimala's head covered, you are left wondering what exactly Mani was trying to say with this look. Perhaps it was a way of incorporating the bohemian vibe that was trending at that time. Still, as unusual as it looked on screen, it did have an impact. As Priya Tanna, editor of Vogue India, says, 'She gave the sari a totally different status by wearing a coat over it... that made it a complete ensemble.'

Throughout the film, Vyjayanthimala's look has a feel of being chic and au courant, yet with a vintage influence. Priya adds, 'The biggest contribution for me in that film was Vyjayanthimala doing nomadic chic. When she sang "Hothon Mein Aisi Baat", the whole outfit had such a nomadic, crafty boho vibe to it, which you see on the runway so often now. Whether it was the chunky silver, or the bangs, or those blousons, the bright colours, the printed skirt – she did gypsy chic really well.' And for mixing grace with the bohemian, Vyjayanthimala will definitely be remembered.

1968
Mumtaz

Brahmachari

Credited Costume Designers
Bhanu Athaiya and Chelaram

This G.P. Sippy production was not only a box-office hit, but also won the Filmfare Best Film Award in 1969. Brahmachari, played by Shammi Kapoor, is on a mission to unite a 'hopelessly in love' Sheetal (Rajshree) with Ravi (Pran) in exchange for money. However, Brahmachari and Sheetal end up falling in love with each other. This doesn't go down well with Ravi. So, in true Bollywood style, there is lots of drama, which includes threats, fights and even kidnapping. Crucial to the plot is the fact that Ravi was also in a relationship with Roopa (Mumtaz), who has his child out of wedlock.

By the time *Brahmachari* hit the screen, Mumtaz was already a seasoned actor. But it was an orange sari from this film that helped turn her into a style icon. Needing to twist her hips for the song '*Aaj Kal Tere Mere Pyaar Ke Charche*', Mumtaz was nervous about dancing in a sari. So her costume designer, Bhanu Athaiya, came up with the perfect solution: a pre-pleated sari with a zip on the side. This flame-coloured sari was the precursor to what is now known as the 'concept sari'. Draped almost like a second skin around the hip and knee, the bottom had a lehenga effect. It was worn low, ensuring it showed off Mumtaz's curves. Bhanu recalls in her book, *The Art of Costume Design*, 'This film was a personal landmark for me because Mumtaz's sparkling personality inspired me to visualize a unique sari dress for a song. I wanted to do full justice to Mumtaz's attractive and free spirit. The lyrics of the song, the mischief in Mumtaz's eyes and the spirit of the dress all came together to create a legend in Hindi commercial cinema.' Traditional gold jewellery, paired with winged eyeliner and bouffant-style hair, both very au courant for the time, gave this look a true feel of high fashion.

Today, most actresses wear a pre-draped sari, but back in the 60s, a sari with a zip caused a sensation, and it became known as the 'Mumtaz sari'. In the 2012 movie *Teri Meri Kahani*, Priyanka Chopra wears an almost identical version of this sari in white while singing '*Jabse Mere Dil Ko Uff*'. This film takes place in three different eras, and that song in particular is set in the 1960s. Referring to the Mumtaz sari makes it instantly connect to that period, truly telling of how iconic that drape is.

1969

Mumtaz

Aadmi Aur Insaan

Credited Costume Designer
Bhanu Athaiya

The cast of this film included Saira Banu, Feroze Khan, Dharmendra and Mumtaz. The plot revolves around Munish Mehra (Dharmendra), whose wealthy friend, Jai Kishan (Feroz Khan), helps him receive a foreign education. However, their friendship turns sour as they both are in love with the same woman, Meena Khanna (Saira Banu). Mumtaz's role may not have been the lead, but she ended up winning the Filmfare Award for Best Supporting Actress for her work in this film.

Rita (Mumtaz), a modern, office-going woman, really enjoys her fashion. Since Mumtaz herself was known for her incredible personal style, she was truly meant for this role of a fashion-conscious professional. She wore off-the-shoulder and form-fitting dresses throughout the film – going from a black dress that looked diaphanous, thanks to a flesh-coloured lining, to an orange off-the-shoulder dress with turquoise blue details. Costume designer Bhanu Athaiya famously used a scarf as an accessory in this movie. It was sometimes tied around Mumtaz's neck and, other times, around her hand, so that she could play with the loose portion.

In *The Art of Costume Design*, Bhanu writes, 'Although Mumtaz was able to portray a village girl as easily as a city-bred one in her career, she was the best in dresses that showed her in an ultra-stylish manner.' The form-fitted, rose-pink dress with its deep neckline, which she wore in the song '*Zindagi Ittefaq Hai*', was considered risqué back then. It was obviously designed to be just a bit sexy, and so was in sync with Mumtaz's character. One cannot ignore how classic that silhouette is today – you can imagine a version of this dress being part of any contemporary woman's evening wardrobe.

1970s & 1980s

1970
Saira Banu

Purab Aur Paschim

Credited Costume Designers
Naseem Banu, B.A. Merchant and Kumud Soni

Produced and directed by Manoj Kumar, the theme of this film is patriotism. Its message was compelling – that gaining independence from the British Raj was not enough, and that you had to feel Indian in your heart. Preeti, played by Saira Banu, is a young woman who was born and raised in England; interestingly enough, Saira herself had studied in private school in London, so she was well matched for this role. In fact, in a 2014 interview with the *Times of India*, the actress talks about how, because she grew up in London, she was also comfortable with the outfits she wore in the film: short dresses and heavy eye make-up, complemented by her blonde hair. The character of Preeti has no feelings or connection to her Indian roots, and her fashion style, taking inspiration from Brigitte Bardot, is a symbol of this.

Preeti falls in love with Bharat (Manoj Kumar), who is as Indian as it gets. As such, she eventually becomes a demure 'Indian' woman, and starts wearing more traditional Indian clothes. She then gives up all her 'foreign' habits, which include smoking and drinking – a cigarette and a glass of wine had almost been accessories for Saira in many parts of this film, be it in the song, *'Twinkle Twinkle Little Star'* in her short red dress, or in *'Hai Preet Jahan Ki Reet Sada'* in her black, shimmering, long body-con dress, accessorized with long dangling earrings and a feather boa.

Arti Sandhu, an associate professor in Fashion Design at the University of Cincinnati, in her book *Indian Fashion: Tradition, Innovation, Style*, says, 'The change from Western to Indian clothing that takes place in many a film like *Purab Aur Paschim* [East and West] (1970) was meant to denote the transition from brash Western modernity to good Indian morals, tradition and spirituality.' This explains how, in that period of Indian cinema, Western dress denoted a woman who was wayward, and traditional Indian dress, the normal choice for the lead, denoted a woman of 'good moral character'.

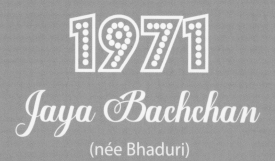

1971
Jaya Bachchan
(née Bhaduri)

Guddi

Credited Costume Designers
M.R. Bhutkar and Mohan

Jaya Bhaduri is an actress known for putting performance before everything. She chose roles where she often had to appear in simple cotton saris and little make-up, but in this film she showed off a more fun and playful side to her style of acting. Guddi (which is Hindi for 'doll'; the character's given name is Kusum) is a schoolgirl infatuated with the actor Dharmendra, who plays himself in the film. Directed by Hrishikesh Mukherjee and written by Gulzar and D.N. Mukherjee, this film is considered one of the actress' finest performances. So memorable was the film that Sonam Kapoor said that it was the look here that inspired her when she had to play a schoolgirl herself in the 2013 film, *Raanjhanaa*. At the promotions of her film, Sonam said, 'The spunkiness that Jayaji's character had in *Guddi*, we needed that. I needed an inspiration, as in real life my schooling was conservative and different. So I needed a starting point. I did watch that film again. It was quite amazing to play this role.'

With her two braids with white ribbons, pinafore with box pleats, white, short-sleeved shirt and white sash belt, Guddi became the stereotype of how a schoolgirl should look. Notably, when Guddi leaves school and transforms into a sari-wearing young woman, often with her hair in a single plait, her body language and stance change, symbolizing the fact that she is now entering adulthood.

1971
Zeenat Aman

Hare Rama Hare Krishna

Credited Costume Designer
Zeenat Aman (for herself)

A film that looked at hippie culture, it was written, produced and directed by Dev Anand, who also played the lead role of Prashant Jaiswal. He needed a woman of real spirit and abandon to play the Westernized and bohemian-living Jasbir, Prashant's long-lost sister. Known also as 'Janice', her hippie name, Jasbir is a rebel. It was Zeenat Aman who was eventually cast, as Dev Anand recalls in his autobiography, *Romancing With Life*, in part because she smoked and had a devil-may-care attitude. She may not have been the filmmaker's first choice, but today it is Zeenat who is the poster girl of the hippie movement of the 1970s in India. Like Janice, Zeenat was brought up in the West and her model-like figure and face ensured that the camera fell in love with her. It was as if the role had been written for her.

It is her pink kurti with marigold garlands worn as necklaces and bracelets, oversized tinted glasses, hoop earrings and long red *tika* from the song 'Dum Maro Dum Mit Jaye Gham' that has become the iconic look of the Indian hippie movement. That song became the anthem for many young Indians at that time. Says author and film critic Udita Jhunjhunwala, 'It's the go-to look when you think of "hippie" in Hindi cinema. Kaizad Gustad paid tribute to it in his movie, *Boom*, as did Rohan Sippy in his film, *Dum Maro Dum*.'

With this film, the young Zeenat Aman (who was just 19 years old), became the figure of the modern, free-spirited Indian woman. As Udita says, 'It was in tune with the times, emulating global trends, which made it instantly aspirational and interesting to Indian audiences. Also, here was an Indian girl indulging in "taboo" things and that rebellion made Janice all the more iconic. The line "Hum ko na roke zamaana, jo chaahenge hum karenge" (the world won't be able to stop us, for we will do what we want) could easily have been the mantra for a generation on the cusp.' While this film came early in Zeenat's career, it was obvious that she was going to be an actress who would willingly take on bold and daring roles.

1971
Asha Parekh

Mera Gaon Mera Desh

Credited Costume Designer
Sudha Parekh

A classic love story between a petty thief and a village girl, this film had Dharmendra and Asha Parekh as its lead pair, with Vinod Khanna as the villain. Ajit (Dharmendra), a small-time thief, has just been released from prison. He moves to a village, where he starts working on a farm and meets Anju (Asha Parekh). They both quickly fall in love. At some point, Ajit decides to take on a dacoit named Jabbar Singh (Vinod Khanna), which leads to Anju being held hostage. The film was a success at the box office, and one of the main attractions was Asha Parekh as Anju. Known as 'the Jubilee Girl' at that time, any project with Asha's presence was a guaranteed commercial success.

In the film's much-appreciated song '*Kuchh Kehta Hai Ye Saawan*', Asha is dressed as a typical village belle, wearing a midi, rani-pink ghagra, a dupatta draped in a peak over her head – reminding you of a classical Manipuri dancer – and a mismatched backless choli with patchwork. One look, and you know this film belongs to the 1970s. The look has a 'more is more' feel to it, which is a typical take on the *gaon ki gori* (village belle) aesthetic for that time. Colourwise, nothing seems as though it belongs together, from the pink, printed dupatta to the mirror work to the multi-coloured choli with a blue bust and colourful pom-poms. For good measure, there is lots of silver jewellery from head to toe. All this sounds like a fashion faux pas, but Asha manages to make it look graceful; perhaps this erratic style of dress was chosen to represent her character's naive yet cheerful and vibrant personality.

Interestingly, the woman behind this look is Asha Parekh's mother, Sudha Parekh. Sudha was what we would today call a 'momager' when it came to her daughter's career. While in her autobiography Asha credits Oscar-winning costume designer Bhanu Athaiya for her celluloid style, Asha worked on many films with her mother in charge of costumes, including *Love in Tokyo* in 1966.

1972
Meena Kumari

Pakeezah

Credited Costume Designer
Meena Kumari (for herself)

Directed by Kamal Amrohi, this is the last film of Meena Kumari, the actress known as 'the Tragedy Queen'. Here, Meena played the courtesans Pakeezah and Nargis. In early twentieth-century Lucknow, Nargis is rejected by the man she loves, Shahabuddin (Ashok Kumar) and passes away shortly after giving birth to their daughter, Sahibjaan. Born out of wedlock, Sahibjaan, like her mother, becomes a courtesan and dancer, and she catches the eye of Salim Ahmed Khan (Raaj Kumar), who changes her name to 'Pakeezah', meaning 'pure'. Meena posthumously received her fourth Filmfare Award for Best Actress for *Pakeezah*. Known to be detail-oriented, she made sure that everything about her title character was looked into, including the costumes, which have all the decadence you would expect in a movie about a nautch (dance) girl. Her orange anarkali from the song '*Chalte Chalte*' remains a classic.

In 2010, *Harper's Bazaar India* decided that the fashion of the film deserved a tribute and asked actress Dia Mirza to step into Meena's shoes for a fashion spread. Styling the shoot was Mohit Rai, who says, 'While I wasn't surprised that the costumes were styled by Meena Kumari (since that was a common format in that day and age), I was quite mesmerized by her attention to detail. Right down to the hair texture, the *alta*, the placement of jewellery, the precision in colours, she was a perfectionist.' The orange and gold combination is one steeped in tradition and worked well with her complexion, dark hair and beautiful eyes, which evoked a kind of inner sadness. As Mohit says, 'The theatricality of the anarkalis and the grandeur of over-accessorizing made for looks that went down in history as classics that serve as inspiration till date.'

1972
Hema Malini

Seeta Aur Geeta

Credited Costume Designers
Leena Daru and Chelaram

A classic story of twins separated at birth, it had Hema Malini in a double role in this Ramesh Sippy film. Seeta, an orphan, is brought up by her wicked aunt. Though they come from an affluent family, she is treated like a servant, much like Cinderella. Geeta, on the other hand, lives in a poor neighbourhood but has a mother who loves her. She is a spirited street performer and her uniform is mirror-worked cholis worn over kitschy skirts, often in bright colours. Fashion played an important role in distinguishing the twins, as they both have different personalities and clothes can help craft this distinction. The lead costume designer for this movie was Leena Daru.

Seeta, who has a much more fragile personality, wears mostly simple cotton saris, except in the scene where she is to meet a prospective groom. She is dressed up by her aunt to look like a complete 'fashion victim'. In the scene, she wears a pink mini dress with bell sleeves, an oversized belt and silver Roman sandals with the straps going up close to her knees. Her make-up looks as if it has been painted on and she even has a temporary heart and arrow tattoo on her face. It makes a mockery out of young women who, at that time, were aping Western fashion without knowing how to carry off the styles. Recalls Ramesh Sippy, 'We needed her to look awkward. She was a girl used to wearing a sari… her aunt wants this proposal to fail and so dresses her to make her feel and look out of place.' Seeta is visibly uncomfortable, tugging her skirt down at every opportunity she gets. This film became one of Hema Malini's most landmark moments and there is always talk of a sequel being made, even though the film is now more than 40 years old.

1973
Dimple Kapadia

Bobby

Credited Costume Designers
Rishi Kapoor (for himself), Stylo, Mani Rabadi and Satyawan

The teenage romance film, *Bobby*, marked the debut of Dimple Kapadia, who was just 16 years old when she won the Filmfare Award for her role as the Catholic Goan girl, Bobby Braganza. This film, directed by Raj Kapoor, was also his son Rishi's first lead role. Rishi played Raj Nath, the good-looking and amiable son of a rich businessman, who falls for Bobby. A story that focuses on teenage love, it was fun, fresh and has since become an essential Bollywood film.

Throughout the film, Bobby wears clothes that play to the fact that she is a Christian girl, and nearly always dons a cross locket on a chain. At the same time, the costume designer, Mani Rabadi, who was responsible for many of the most fashion-savvy films of the time, kept things full of spunk in this film. Dimple possessed a strong sense of body confidence that was not associated with a young star from Indian cinema in that era, and was able to carry off every look. Wearing a bright red bikini in the pool scene, she became an instant sex symbol.

Though she was meant to be playing a fisherman's daughter, her outfits were very fashion-forward for that time – this is typical of a Raj Kapoor film. Since her character was not from an affluent family, nothing was too glamorous, yet that only made Dimple's look appeal to many young women of that time. Surprisingly, it is not the bikini that *Bobby* is remembered for, but the polka-dot blouse tied above the waist and worn with a short, black, front-buttoned skirt. It evoked an image that was naughty yet innocent, demure yet sensual – and is also the outfit that Bobby wears for her first kiss with Raj. This outfit made another appearance in the 2010 film, *Once Upon a Time in Mumbaai*. Prachi Desai portrays Mumtaz, a shop girl, who wears a replica of 'the Bobby outfit'. Such is the impact of this ensemble that, almost 40 years later, it is still a major point of reference.

1973
Zeenat Aman

Yaadon Ki Baaraat

Credited Costume Designers
Leena Shah, Rose Bleu and Bilquis Khan

The flick is about three brothers, Shankar, Vijay and Ratan (Dharmendra, Vijay Arora and Tariq Khan) who witness the murder of their parents at a young age and eventually end up being raised separately. It has a bit of everything – action, thrill and romance – and so is considered to be a trendsetter for the masala genre of Indian cinema. Zeenat Aman played the rich man's daughter, Sunita, who falls in love with Vijay, a man from a much different financial background. Working on the costumes for the film were Leena Shah, Rose Bleu and Bilquis Khan. It was common practice then to have more than one designer working on the film, along with the directors and lead actors, who were also often very involved in the costumes.

This film released the same year that model-turned-actress Parveen Babi made her debut in *Charitra*, marking the start of comparisons between the two. These two were seen as actresses who represented a new generation of young women in India – those who dared to live life on their own terms, yet at heart were women whom you could take home to your mother. Together they changed the image of the Indian heroine. Film critic and author Udita Jhunjhunwala explains, 'Zeenat, like Parveen Babi, captured the zeitgeist – she represented the adventurous, confident and glamorous Indian woman who could blend Indian-ness with Western manners. She brought a cosmopolitanism to the Indian woman and broke away from images of the dutiful sari-clad wife or sister.'

It is the song 'Chura Liya Hai' that was Zeenat's most memorable fashion moment in this film. Wearing a white palazzo jumpsuit with a black choker, she looked thoroughly modern and sophisticated. It is this look that actress Sonakshi Sinha paid homage to on the sets of *Nach Baliye*, and it looked as modern now as it did then. Zeenat's look was also the perfect match for the beautiful melody and lyrics by music director R.D. Burman. While the outfit covered much of her skin, it was fitted till the waist and had a V-neck, thus managing to be both sensual and graceful.

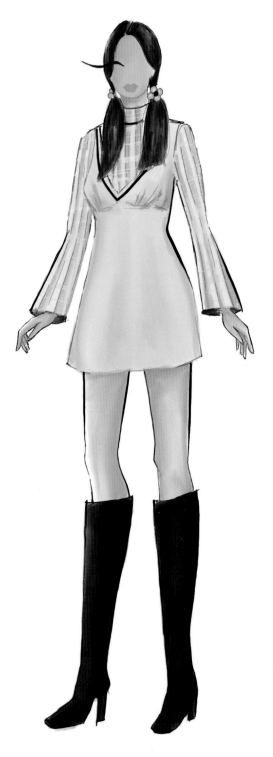

1975
Neetu Singh

Khel Khel Mein

Credited Costume Designers
**Leena Daru, Shalini Shah, Mani Rabadi, New Stylo,
Super Tailors, Glamour and Kachins**

This was quite a year for Indian films. Action and drama films like *Sholay*, *Deewar* and *Aandhi* were all critical and commercial blockbusters, though this romantic comedy with its on-screen-off-screen couple, Rishi Kapoor and Neetu Singh, managed to hold its own. It is a fun, playful and romantic film, and is based on the novel *Good Children Don't Kill* by Louis Thomas. Rishi Kapoor, Rakesh Roshan and Neetu Singh played Ajay, Vikram and Nisha – three good friends in college who enjoy playing pranks on others. However, one prank goes awfully wrong and they find themselves in the middle of a murder mystery where Vikram ends up dead, and the movie takes an unexpected twist. As the story unfolds, Nisha and Ajay begin to fall in love with each other.

In the movie, it is impossible to miss the peppy and trendy costumes worn by the lead actors, especially Nisha in her short skirts and Ajay in his wing-collar shirts. Working on the film in the costume department were two of the leading costume designers of the day, Mani Rabadi and Leena Daru.

Neetu's look, in many aspects, spoke to how young people wanted to dress in that decade. It turned Neetu (not known at that point for her fashion sense) into a style icon, mainly due to her look in the song *'Ek Main Aur Ek Tu'*. She wore a short, powder-blue, sleeveless dress with a V-neck over a bell-sleeved shirt with black boots. Her hair was tied into two loose pigtails and fastened with flower hair-ties. Sounds a little thrown together? That was the point of the film, which was about being carefree at that stage of life where you just want to have fun.

1975
Hema Malini

Sholay

Credited Costume Designers
Shalini Shah, Chelaram, Kachins, Robe Stylo and New Stylo

'Indian film history can be divided into *Sholay* BC and *Sholay* AD', filmmaker Shekhar Kapoor famously said of this film. Directed by Ramesh Sippy, it was called a 'Curry Western', and is still considered to be one of Indian cinema's most important films. Who can forget Basanti (Hema Malini), the village belle, dancing to save her true love, Veeru (Dharmendra), from the dacoit Gabbar Singh (Amjad Khan). Basanti twirls and twirls and is eventually made to dance on broken glass by Gabbar Singh. Not even the fresh blood of her feet, luridly matching the pink of her ghagra skirt and choli, stops her from going until she finally becomes too weak to move. In interviews, Hema Malini says that when people meet her, they still call her 'Basanti'.

Though the film was shot in South India's Karnataka and Hema Malini herself is South Indian, it was a distinctively North Indian story. Says Ramesh Sippy, '*Sholay*'s location is a fictional place, but it is somewhere in North India and so Basanti's clothes are representative of that.' Hema wore a mash-up of regional styles from North and West India. Her brashness was matched by her kitsch costumes, which included some attention-seeking, jingling silver anklets and lots of mirror work on her vibrant traditional ensembles that were accessorized with mixed and matched jewellery. A daredevil who rides a horse cart, Basanti is very spirited, and her colourful and short ghagra cholis go with her personality.

Her hair, worn with curls tied in a loose up-do, often with flowers adorning them, created quite a style statement at that time. In fact, Bhawana Somaaya, noted film journalist, critic and historian, says that while Hema's clothing was certainly memorable, 'what made the difference was the hairstyle; she ties her hair on the side like the messy bun of Deepika Padukone in present time.' Women from all over India quickly wanted to replicate that style. 'I can't remember how we came up with that hairstyle; it just was different from looks in other films and looked good on her', recalls Ramesh. And while the *gaon ki gori* (village belle) aesthetic may not be as strong a force as it once was in Indian cinema, it still has a presence. Four decades later, all on-screen village girls are compared to Hema Malini's Basanti, be it how they act or how they look. As Ramesh says of Basanti's look: 'It just has a timeless quality.'

1977

Parveen Babi

Amar Akbar Anthony

Credited Costume Designers

Mani Rabadi, Leena Daru, Kachins, Super Tailor

This Manmohan Desai film stars Amitabh Bachchan, Vinod Khanna and Rishi Kapoor as three brothers who are separated at an early age, and find themselves adopted by different families. Amar Khanna (Vinod Khanna) is Hindu, Akbar Illhabadi (Rishi Kapoor) is Muslim and Anthony Gonsalves (Amitabh Bachchan) is Christian. Parveen Babi played Jenny, a Christian, Shabana Azmi played Lakshmi, a Hindu, and Neetu Singh played Dr. Salma, a Muslim. What they wore represented each of their religions in a somewhat stereotypical manner. As the film was premised on the importance of religious tolerance, however, this overt style of dressing worked well with the script. *Amar Akbar Anthony* remains one of the most important films of the 1970s, and was remade in Tamil, Telugu and Malayalam.

In the film's most important song, *'My Name is Anthony Gonsalves'*, Parveen, who was already considered one of film's glam girls, wore a strappy, red maxi dress – a style that was popular at that time. Belted at the waist, it had black and gold detailing, and a black bead necklace that helped enhance these details. A red rose in her hair was a signature look, and mirrored the black rose on her belt. Not the most innovative of designs, but it was very much what young women of the time wanted to wear for a night out on the town. Only they might have opted for shoes – Parveen, in this dance number, was barefoot.

Mani Rabadi, the costume designer of this film, was known for her love of glamour, and this certainly complemented the cinematic style of Manmohan Desai, a pioneer of the 'masala' film genre. The red-panelled strapless dress thus spoke to how 'high fashion' was perceived by mainstream India in the 70s. Still, Parveen's make-up was kept fairly natural, with her impactful kohl-rimmed eyes standing out the most.

The film came out just after Parveen became the first Indian film star to appear on the cover of *Time* magazine for a story called 'Asia's Frenetic Film Scene', and was chosen as the modern face of Indian cinema. Fittingly, perhaps, as she is also *Amar Akbar Antony's* most visibly modern character.

1977
Shabana Azmi

Amar Akbar Anthony

Credited Costume Designers
Mani Rabadi, Leena Daru, Kachins and Super Tailor

Playing the Hindu female lead, Lakshmi, was Shabana Azmi, who of course wore a sari for many scenes in the film. Lakshmi is a live-wire who is happy to use her womanly ways to try to steal money while hitching a ride from a passer-by (who turns out to be police inspector Amar Khanna, played by Vinod Khanna). As feisty as she seems, Lakshmi has been forced into a life of crime by her stepfamily. In this scene, she tries to con Amar, who later becomes her love interest. She wore yellow bell bottoms and a bold floral top, knotted at the stomach to reveal just a flash of skin. Could you get more 1970s than this?

There is a sort of fashion naiveté to this outfit, and that is what made it so appealing. In fact, it reflected what many young women thought was the epitome of style at the time. The average woman had her clothes stitched by a tailor after buying fabric from a local market, and this was the reference many soon began taking to their tailors.

As the inspector falls for Lakshmi and takes her into his home to save her from her wicked stepbrother and stepmother, you note that she now mostly wears demure saris, perhaps to show her transformation from being a petty thief to a 'good girl'. This helped her initial bell-bottom look stand out even more. In a bridesmaid scene, however, she wears a sugary-pink dress; perhaps the shocking choice of colour was chosen to show she was not happy to be a bridesmaid to the reluctant bride, Jenny (Parveen Babi). Luckily, the bridesmaid dress, which was a bit of an eyesore, did not filter down to the street like the bell bottoms and floral crop blouse did.

1977
Hema Malini

Dream Girl

Credited Costume Designers
Mani Rabadi, Bhanu Athaiya, Sewak Ram and New Stylo

From her first film, Hema Malini was known as India's 'Dream Girl'. In the title song, she wears a red apsara outfit, which is first shown on a painting and then on her. In the movie, the rich and handsome Anupam Verma (Dharmendra) buys the painting from a street vendor and believes that the woman in it is his 'dream girl'. Two leading costume designers are credited for their work in this film: Mani Rabadi and Bhanu Athaiya.

Apsaras, according to Hindu mythology, were nymphs who were born to dance for the gods. The choice of this apasara-style of outfit for Hema's opening sequence complemented her talent as a trained Bharatanatyam dancer and her sheer beauty; helpfully, it also showed off her curves. She was adorned with plenty of ethnic gold jewellery and heavy make-up (including green eye shadow). The song was shot with many effects, so it indeed feels like it is part of a dream. Like most Bollywood dance numbers, it featured multiple outfit changes – an ethereal white choli worn over a skirt with silver embroidery and slits on both sides, and a headband and jewellery to complete the look, is followed by a floral outfit that may have been inspired by Hawaiian hula dancers. But it is the red apsara outfit that was on promotional billboards, and continues to be the image that is most associated with the film. Fast-forward to present day and all the costumes seem almost gimmicky, but this was very much the style of the time. While Hema Malini might be known for her elegant chiffon saris today, she will always be remembered as the apsara of *Dream Girl*.

1978
Helen

Don

Credited Costume Designers
Mani Rabadi and Smt. S. Irani

This crime thriller starring Amitabh Bachchan and Zeenat Aman in the lead roles quickly became a blockbuster. It spurred remakes in Telugu, Tamil and Malayalam, and in 2006, Farhan Akhtar paid homage to film with his 'redux' Hindi version, *Don: The Chase Begins*.

In the original movie, Helen's cabaret number in the song '*Yeh Mera Dil*' was the film's most sizzling moment. In this song, Kamini (Helen), whose fiancé was killed by Don (Amitabh Bachchan), is disguised as the seductress Sonia. She tries to distract Don so that the police can catch up with them and arrest the mobster. The original item girl, Helen exuded sex appeal, and her skimpy costumes were part of her trademark. Her nails were talon-shaped and painted burgundy. Two large cocktail rings and a bracelet studded with red stones adorned her hands.

Though she often wore body stockings, in '*Yeh Mera Dil*', her white, low-cut top teamed with a low-waisted skirt with long slits left little to the imagination. Working on this film's costumes was Mani Rabadi; she and Helen had a history of working on clothes that were unexpected, over the top and in the realm of the burlesque. If anyone else but this showgirl had worn them, they would seem garish, but Helen knew how to keep it risqué yet classy. The outfit was embellished with a red stone border, and she wore blue contact lenses and silver sandals – she wanted to make a bold statement. Interestingly, when Kareena Kapoor reprised the song in Farhan Akhtar's 2006 version, she wore a gold dress with slits, and was actually more covered up than Helen.

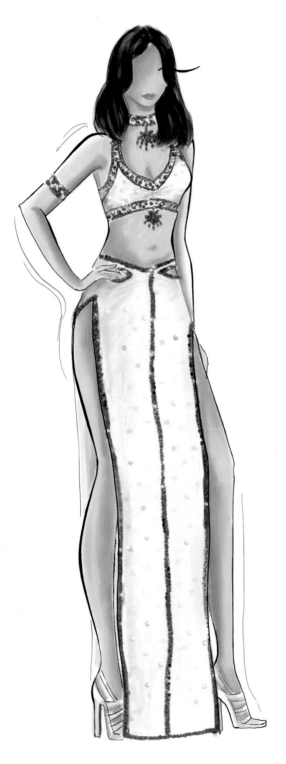

1978
Zeenat Aman

Satyam Shivam Sundaram

Credited Costume Designers
Bhanu Athaiya, Burlingtons, Super Tailor and Satyawan

In this Raj Kapoor flick, which was considered controversial at the time, Zeenat Aman plays Roopa, a priest's daughter with an angelic voice. Unfortunately for her, as a child, an accident scarred one side of her face, which she covers with a *pallu* for most of the movie. Shashi Kapoor plays the handsome engineer Rajeev, who falls in love with her after hearing her sing. He only finds out about her scars after he marries her and feels cheated; he is convinced that he has married the wrong woman. Although the movie was widely criticized at the time of its release for showing too much skin, it was a box-office success.

Zeenat's costumes ranged from simple village girl outfits to apsara-inspired, cabaret-style costumes for fantasy sequences. Costume designer Bhanu Athaiya said that this film was one of her most challenging assignments due to the sharp contrasts in the presentation of Zeenat. She recalls in her book, *The Art of Costume Design*, 'Zeenat's character was that of a priest's daughter, so the entire look had to be acceptable from an "Indian" point of view.' This film allowed the former model and Miss India Asia Pacific winner to display the complete confidence she had in front of the camera. Even today, the scene under the waterfall in the song '*Bhor Bhaye Panghat Pe*', where she wears a white cotton sari, is considered one of Indian cinema's most erotic moments.

The 'wet sari' had become a unique way to portray sensuality since censor boards in India have always had a conservative take on showing women's skin. Zeenat wore India's most traditional form of dress, the sari, and yet there is no question that there is something tantalizing about the sari, especially when it is diaphanous, white and translucent. While some criticized this scene as merely trying to titillate, it was clearly a very artful way of exploring a woman's sensual side. Nandini Bhalla, the editor of *Cosmopolitan India*, observes, 'The white sari, of course, plays a crucial role here, adding innocence to the scene… a garment and colour considered chaste, feminine and traditional, allowing spectators both in-theatre and in-film to view these women as accidentally sensual, instead of wilfully arousing.'

1980
Simi Garewal

Karz

Credited Costume Designers
**Bhavana Munim, Bhanu Athaiya, Satyawan, Kachins
and New Stylo**

In this Subash Ghai action film about reincarnation, Simi Garewal plays Kamini, alongside Raj Kiran as Ravi Verma, the well-off husband Kamini kills for an inheritance. Ravi Verma is later reborn as a musician, Monty, played by Rishi Kapoor. When Ravi remembers how he and his family were wronged by Kamini, he begins to look for her.

Simi was an actress known for her bold and offbeat role choices. Having grown up in London, she had a Western outlook on all things, including fashion, and was considered a true trendsetter. In fact, some of the clothes used in *Karz* came from Simi's own wardrobe. Of course, at first she was apprehensive about playing Kamini, and it took the director more than a year to persuade her to take on the role with its many shades of grey. Kamini is a woman who likes to be powerful in the decade of power dressing – the 1980s. Yet she is feminine and has a softness to her. All these aspects of the character were taken into consideration. 'I remember in the last scene, where she wears a black-and-white kaftan and confesses that she did kill Ravi, I wanted her to wear black and white to signify that she was finally admitting to the evil [the black] in her', says Simi.

In one of the early parts of the film, when Kamini drives her husband off a cliff near a small temple of Goddess Kali, she wears a faux leather jacket and leather driving gloves. The white polo neck features strongly and at that time was considered the epitome of chic. There is also the fur hat and fur-trimmed jacket she wears in the car with Monty, and the oversized feather-trimmed teal shawl with art-deco style jewellery as she watches Monty sing '*Ek Haseena Thi*'. The mirror-work trimmed, black chiffon dress with the belt, worn as she lounges at home and answers the phone, came from Parmeshwar Godrej's store, Dancing Silks, which Simi went to quite often at the time. She says, 'It was one of the first stores in India where you could buy Western clothes and also fabrics. I remember I saw the mirror-work there, which was used in such a modern way, and so I asked Bhanu to make a dress using the fabric.' Bhanu Athaiya was the costume designer of the film, and was described by Simi as 'a genius, a scholar, a true fountain of knowledge who researched every detail.'

Rekha

Khubsoorat

Credited Costume Designers
New Stylo, Leena Daru and Maqsood

Rekha believes that it is *Khubsoorat*, directed by Hrishikesh Mukherjee, that made her known for her acting; she won her first Filmfare Best Actress award for her performance. *Khubsoorat* takes a wholesome and light look at marriage, family and relationships, with Rekha playing the lead role of Manju, a woman full of joie de vivre. Manju's elder sister, Anju, played by Aradhana, marries into the Gupta family, who have a traditional view as to how family life should be. Manju falls in love with one of their sons, played by Rakesh Roshan, much to the disapproval of the matriarch.

Leena Daru worked on the film's modest but memorable costumes, but more than the clothes in general, it is Rekha's signature look that is remembered. With her middle-parted hair, two braids and clips on the side, the look is neat and simple. Her make-up is mainly in tones of bronze and brown and keeps up with the trends of the time; it is more toned down than in many of Rekha's other films. Hrishikesh Mukherjee never believed in glamour, and Manju's look goes well with his style of filmmaking, be it in the coral belted dress she wears as she teases her sister on the upcoming *rishta* or the black-and-white checked kurta she wears with silver *kolhapuri* chappals when she dresses as a boy for the comical song 'Saare Niyam Tod Do'. Her style really looks like it belongs to an everyday young woman. In many scenes, she wears printed silk saris with modest elbow-length blouses and small hoop or stud earrings. This no-fuss wardrobe enhanced Rekha's measured performance and you cannot help but fall in love with Manju.

The film was remade in 2014 with Sonam Kapoor and Fawad Khan, but its storyline was altered. In this film, Sonam's character, Mili, is a professional physiotherapist and Fawad is a prince, Vikram Singh Rathore. There is nothing 'middle class' about this new script. Though Sonam did wear Rekha's two braids, her wardrobe was more fashion-forward and eclectic. You can tell there was much emphasis on what she wore, and Sonam's wardrobe did become a talking point with the fashion media. And yet it makes you appreciate the effortless and straightforwardness of Rekha's look in the original even more. It is undoubtedly the modesty of the original that made it so special.

1980
Zeenat Aman

Qurbani

Credited Costume Designers
**Sheikh Akber and Sheikh Lal (wardrobe in-charge),
Ram's Stylo, New Stylo and Jawahar Dress Wala**

'When you think of disco in India, it is impossible not to think of "*Aap Jaisa Koi*", the song featuring Zeenat Aman in the iconic red dress', says film critic and author Udita Jhunjhunwala. By this time, Zeenat had established herself as a style icon, and in *Qurbani* she played the glamorous cabaret singer, Sheela, who is the love interest of two men (Rajesh, played by Feroz Khan, and Amar, played by Vinod Khanna), both of whom have a connection to organized crime.

In the movie, Zeenat lip-syncs to '*Aap Jaisa Koi*', a song inspired by the music of Euro-Caribbean band, Boney M. In a red dress with generous side cut-outs and long side slits, Zeenat dazzled like a disco ball. Her straight long hair with a large red rose on the side added a memorable dash of femininity.

'In a time much before fashion glossies and Instagram, followers of Hindi cinema took their fashion cues from the movies. What set Zeenat Aman apart from her contemporaries was her inherent Westernization and her confidence with her curves', explains Udita. Zeenat was a former model who had spent time growing up in Germany, and had a Western approach that made her different from other leading ladies of her time. For most of her career, she was compared to her colleague and fellow sex symbol Parveen Babi, but when you think of a stand-out 1980s disco diva moment, it is the image of Zeenat that instantly comes to mind.

1981
Rekha

Silsila

Credited Costume Designers
Pamela Chopra, Jennifer Kapoor and Leena Daru

This Yash Chopra film features Amitabh Bachchan, Jaya Bachchan and Rekha, and is said to be based on the real-life love triangle between them. It was the last film in which Rekha appeared on screen with her rumoured off-screen love, Mr. Bachchan. Despite this backdrop, the film did not perform well at the box office. Ironically, though, it is considered a cult classic today, thanks to the subject matter, visualization and solid performances.

In the movie, both leading ladies are seen in multiple beautiful saris that reflect the individual role each plays. Shobha (Jaya Bachchan), a wronged wife, has a softer and more docile character than Chandni (Rekha), and dons classic looks featuring rich hand-woven drapes that are teamed with more modest, half-sleeved blouses. Chandni, who is 'the other woman', wears chiffon and crepe saris in solid colours, with lots of cap-sleeved blouses. Jaya's saris were often stronger in colour and had patterns, draped in a looser manner than those of Rekha, who was known for her sensuous curves. There are some fine examples of ikats and Benarasi saris in this film. Rekha's berry-coloured lips were all the rage at that time, but it is the way the sari is portrayed, with beauty and unique style and meaning, that makes *Silsila* an important fashion film.

In an interview with *Hindustan Times*, Yash Chopra said, 'Rekha and I worked hard on *Silsila*. For the songs, she used most of her own jewellery.' Although Pamela Chopra (his wife), Jennifer Kapoor and Leena Daru are officially credited with working on the film as dress designers, it seems that both actress and director were also very involved with the costumes.

1981
Rekha

Umrao Jaan

Credited Costume Designer
Subhashini Ali

A true classic, *Umrao Jaan* had Rekha looking majestic in every scene. Set in nineteenth-century Awadh, the movie is based on the Urdu novel *Umrao Jaan Ada* by Mirza Hadi Ruswa, and tells the tragic tale of a courtesan, Umrao Jaan (Rekha), who was sold into the profession as a young girl. The dances, the sets, the music and the lyrics had a feel of poetic beauty; you can tell the film was a labour of love for its director and producer, Muzaffar Ali. He took a great interest in the fashion stylings of the film, and worked alongside his then wife, Subhashini Ali, who is credited as the official costume designer of the film.

Says Muzaffar, 'The whole journey of *Umrao Jaan* was really a search for fabrics. I got this inspiration from my mother because she was very passionate about clothes and fabric. And most of the clothes you see in *Umrao Jaan* are dug up from her old wardrobe.' Where there is opulence, there is also elegance, which was a balance that he worked hard to ensure. Muzaffar says he sourced the fabrics from Benares with the guidance of the owner of the Indian Textiles Co., whose store and showroom were and still are in the Taj Mahal Palace Hotel, Mumbai. He says, 'It is owned by Sushil Kumar, a great connoisseur of shawls; he gave me a lot of his shawls and he led me through Benares like no other person can. He was so passionate about Benares.'

Wearing a white anarkali layered with jewellery in the song '*In Aankhon Ki Masti*', Rekha mesmerized audiences. This jewellery was a mix of sourced jewellery and Rekha's own; as an actress, she was well known for using her personal wardrobe on film sets. Says Muzaffar about this iconic celluloid moment, 'I'm so driven by poetry. So the poetry of clothes and the poetry of character is integrated into a cinematic statement.' This classic film was later remade in 2006 by J.P. Dutta with Abhishek Bachchan and Aishwarya Rai Bachchan, but it did not quite have the soul and splendour of the original.

1982
Parveen Babi

Yeh Nazdeekiyan

Credited Costume Designers
Leena Daru, Sulakshana, Burlingtons, Kachins and Badasaab

This film earned Parveen Babi the nickname 'India's Bo Derek'. It explored extra-marital relationships – a subject matter that was considered bold, and which certainly needed an actress who had a devil-may-care attitude to essay the role of the 'other' woman. Vinod Pande cast Parveen Babi, an actress known for her bohemian approach to her career and life. She played Kiran, a model who has an affair with the married head of an advertising agency, Sunil Verma, played by Marc Zuber. While the critics called the film 'clichéd', it is famous for giving Indian cinema one of its most important bikini moments, and that can be credited to the woman who wore the two-piece swimsuit.

As Parveen runs out of the sea in a printed bikini, she captures the essence of a woman who is truly free-spirited. Narresh Kukreja is the co-creative director of Shivan and Narresh, one of India's best-known designer swimwear and resort labels today, and he says, 'Parveen Babi in a bikini, sprinting along the beach with roaring waves splashing against her body, is one of the most iconic swimwear scenes in Indian cinema. This sensuous spectacle set a momentous precedence for the film industry to celebrate the golden curves and proportions of the Indian figure.' Though Parveen wore a sarong to make the look seem more modest, the scene is full of erotic energy. It remains one of the bikini's most referred-to moments in Indian fashion history.

It is also an example of how films can help empower the fashion industry. While neither of the men behind Shivan and Narresh was born when this film released, Narresh says that this scene from the movie still serves as an inspiration. Explains the designer, 'It prompted us to work towards building body confidence in women and help them take pride in their curvaceous figures while donning body-con silhouettes.'

Parveen was not the first Indian actress to wear a bikini on the big screen – Dimple Kapadia and Zeenat Aman had both previously worn two-piece swimsuits. But there was something about the way she ran down that beach that had Parveen becoming India's premier pin-up girl.

1982
Parveen Babi

Namak Halaal

Credited Costume Designer
Xerxes Bhathena

This Prakesh Mehra action-comedy film had a stellar cast that included Amitabh Bachchan, Smita Patil, Shashi Kapoor, Suresh Oberoi and Waheeda Rehman. It revolves around Arjun (Amitabh Bachchan), whose father, Bhim Singh (Suresh Oberoi), is killed. Arjun works as a bell boy at a hotel owned by Raja Kumar (Shashi Kapoor); its manager is the son of the man who killed his father, and who now plans to kill Raja. Providing the heat in this film were Parveen Babi as Nisha, a singer and dancer at Raja's hotel, and the film's leading lady, Smita Patil, whose costumes were designed by her sister, Manya Patil Seth. Xerxes Bhathena, a designer that Parveen often collaborated with, worked on this film.

Parveen, not surprisingly, kept it glamorous and Western in this film. The song '*Raat Baaki Baat Baki*' is proof of this. In her shimmering, fitted black gown with a high back slit, metallic tassel earrings and straight black hair, she made you sit up and look at her. Memorably, Parveen made Bappi Lahiri's disco music sensual yet full of finesse. She had no problem being the object of desire, but then again she *was* also playing an alluring female assassin. This was the peak of the Parveen Babi–Zeenat Aman era of Indian cinema: these two former models had become the glam girls of Bollywood and changed the rules completely. With them around, there was no need for vamps and cabaret numbers – they could be the heroine and the vamp, all in one.

Little did anyone know that this was to be one of the last times Parveen would set the screen on fire. The year after the release of this film, she went into a self-imposed exile from Bollywood and left India.

1985
Mandakini

Ram Teri Ganga Maili

Credited Costume Designers
Kachins, Bhanu Athaiya and Satyawan

This is Raj Kapoor's last film and its lead was played by his youngest son, Rajiv Kapoor, as the suave, city-dwelling Narendra. The film was one of 1985's highest grossers at the box office. A young Mandakini played a village belle, Ganga, who catches the eye of Narendra. He marries her and then leaves her, and she soon finds that she is pregnant. En route to find the father of her child, she is abducted and molested and finally finds herself at the mercy of a powerful politician. The film is evidently a work of social commentary, but this is not what made this film famous. Its social message found itself overshadowed by a white sari.

This scene, reminiscent of the one in *Satyam Shivam Sundaram*, was probably Mandakini's most important role during her short and highly controversial career. Interestingly, in her book, *The Art of Costume Design*, costume designer Bhanu Athaiya only talks of the village girl costumes she designed for this film, which mainly revolved around the ghagra skirt. She does not even mention the white cotton sari that created such a scandal back in the mid-1980s.

It remains a mystery as to how the Indian Censor Board did not cut the bathing scene from the movie. Wearing a diaphanous white sari, Mandakini bathes under a waterfall and her breasts are clearly visible. Little is left to the imagination, yet there is something innocent and almost virginal about the way she looks. The white is obviously chosen for this reason, and the raining water is, of course, a reference to fertility.

This film cemented Raj Kapoor's position in Indian film history as the architect of the 'wet sari'. Nandini Bhalla, editor of *Cosmopolitan India*, points out, that 'the white sari – more specifically, the wet white sari – was Bollywood's way of titillating the Indian male gaze, while also keeping his conservative prudishness in mind. Because while both Raj Kapoor films feature nudity, it is accidental – with a touch of voyeurism. Both "village" heroines, with white, virginal saris hugging their curves, are unaware that they are being watched by "city" men.'

1986
Dimple Kapadia

Janbaaz

Credited Costume Designers
Badasaab, New Stylo and Madhav

This Feroz Khan film takes a look at the more hedonistic side of the 1980s, with a plot that involves drugs and pre-marital sex. It is a *desi* take on the 1946 classical Western film, *Duel in the Sun*. Dimple Kapadia played Reshma, an independent-minded young woman whose father is murdered by a drug lord. She comes to live with the Singhs at their plush farmhouse. It is here that she falls in love with Amar (Anil Kapoor), a debonair Casanova. Dimple's character is brazen, but she is a romantic at heart.

Feroz, often called the 'Clint Eastwood of the East', was heavily involved in the styling of his film, from the sets to the fashion; his own style of dressing was quite flamboyant. Working with him on the costumes was his wife at the time, Sundari Khan, though she is not officially credited. 'This film had a "Wild, Wild West" feel. It worked with its environment set in a farmhouse, with the horses and the stables. I chose earthy colours to work with the outdoorsy setting', recalls Sundari.

In *Janbaaz*, it is Rekha, in the item song, '*Pyaar Do Pyaar Lo*', who provides the diva element. But the most memorable moment in the film lies in the song '*Tera Saath Hai Kitna*', where Dimple wears an orange off-shoulder top tucked into a knee-length embroidered skirt, teamed with long boots and chunky gold jewellery that ensures there is some glamour to her style. Sundari had this outfit especially tailored – a 1980s take on boho-chic – though the boots and some of the accessories came from Dimple's own wardrobe.

Dimple's look suited the fact that Reshma was projected as a sophisticated beauty, and not overtly sexual. 'Since Dimple is more soft-looking… I wanted to ensure the clothes did not overpower her. Plus, Dimple herself has a great sense of style', explains Sundari. With her signature voluminous locks (except for one or two scenes where she has permed curls), Dimple's natural beauty is made the most of in *Janbaaz*.

1987
Smita Patil

Mirch Masala

Credited Costume Designer
Archana Shah

A film with bold subject matter needed an actress of substance, and that is truly what Smita Patil was. This Ketan Mehta film is based in Kutch in the last decade of the British Raj, and playing the character of Sonabai was Smita. This village woman, whose husband is travelling, catches the attention of Subedar, the local tax collector, portrayed by Naseeruddin Shah. When he propositions her, Smita runs to a factory where women grind chillies (*mirch*), for protection, but that does not stop Naseeruddin's pursuit of her. The movie is about a woman who stands up to sexual harassment, along with the help of the women of the *mirch* factory.

The costume designer for the film was Ketan Shah's then wife Archana Shah. She is the author of a book on the textiles and traditions of Kutch, *Shifting Sands*, which explains how the costume design of this film was such an exacting process. Smita's mirror-worked, low-backed *kapadus* (the type of blouse worn by women of that region) and tie-dye cotton *odhinis,* mainly in the colour of spices, were true to the way women of this region dressed. This was also in sync with the storyline of *Mirch Masala*. Archana recalls that she picked up most of Smita's outfits and jewellery from Kutch and then carefully altered them to fit her.

For fashion designer Nachiket Barve, a National Institute of Design graduate working on costumes for Marathi films, including a film based on the celebrated Maratha warrior, *Taanaji*, in which Ajay Devgn plays the lead, this film remains an inspiration. He says, 'The costumes steered away from the trap of typecasting the alluring village woman as a stereotypical sex object by carefully controlling the authenticity of the costumes and relying on the actor's prowess to still carry forward the narrative. They become an integral part of making it a successful film. For an urban and progressive actress to appear so real in the film, the credit goes to the immensely gifted actor, but also the costume and make-up designers.' He adds, 'To see an everyday-looking woman stand up for herself and not allow sexual harassment passively… it is the precursor of the #MeToo movement we are seeing three decades later.'

1988
Rekha

Khoon Bhari Maang

Credited Costume Designers

**Harish Kale, Pramila Roshan, Kachins, Madhav Tailors, Leena Daru,
Abu Jani–Sandeep Khosla**

This is 1980s excess at its best. In the lead role was one of Indian cinema's most enduring style icons, Rekha – she stars in the film as a meek and trusting widow, Aarti Verma, who has a large scar on her face. When her doting and wealthy father dies, she becomes an heiress. In walks Sanjay Verma (Kabir Bedi), who is actually the boyfriend of Nandini (Sonu Walia), a close friend of Aarti's and a beautiful model. Sanjay enlists Nandini and they hatch a plot to trick Aarti into marrying him. A day after the wedding, they try to kill her by throwing her into crocodile-infested waters. Aarti survives but is disfigured, and after extensive plastic surgery, she is transformed into the glamorous Jyoti. She then becomes a model working alongside Nandini, and plans her revenge. This Rakesh Roshan movie was inspired by the popular Australian television mini-series *Return to Eden*, and Rekha's look as Jyoti is that of Grace Jones meets Joan Collins from Joan's role in the iconic 1980s American television show, *Dynasty*.

The big shoulders, the bling, the lamé, the turbans, the oversized sunglasses and the in-your-face make-up – this no-holds-barred wardrobe consisted of everything that made the 1980s the 1980s. Sandeep Khosla, who worked on some costumes for the film (mainly for Sonu Walia), recalls that Rekha was very involved in what she wore. In retrospect, it might remind you of everything that was wrong with fashion in that decade, but it made such an impact at the time by bringing the strongest international trends of that day to the screen. As Nonita Kalra, editor of *Harper's Bazaar India*, says, 'Nothing succeeds like excess in India and Rekha epitomized it. Her film career was punctuated as much by her style as it was by her performances. Every time Rekha transformed her style, it impacted her career, because she understood the value of getting into character. She was a true chameleon.' The way Rekha transformed from the somewhat frumpy Aarti to super-glam Jyoti was a complete on-screen make-over. Adds Nonita, 'It all emphasized that you can own fashion and it doesn't have to define you. In my book, she was the first fashion rebel.' This film made many women in India realize that they too could embrace these high-fashion looks and encouraged them to be adventurous with their personal style.

Madhuri Dixit

Tezaab

Credited Costume Designers
Kachins, Madhav's Men's Modes, Mani Rabadi, Badasaab, Leena Daru, Sangeeta Chopra and Ram Stylo

One cannot help but remember the bright pink, one-shoulder blouse, and the multi-coloured, panelled, midi-length bohemian skirt that Madhuri Dixit wore in *Tezaab* for the song, *'Ek Do Teen'*. Leena Daru was the costume designer behind this memorable look. In this movie that changed the course of her career, Madhuri played Mohini, a nightclub dancer, who is her stepfather's meal ticket.

With the curly hair, yellow-sequined headband and excessive pink make-up, this look stands for all that was wrong with fashion at that time. Yet, the song is iconic, and bringing that 'X factor' was Madhuri herself. The actress, who is a trained Kathak dancer, moved with great elegance to the music. While appearing on Simi Garewal's television show, *Rendezvous with Simi Garewal*, Madhuri recalls how it was this song that gave her a taste of what it meant to be famous, as everywhere she went people would start shouting, 'Mohini, Mohini' to her. It was a major turning point in her career.

This song made a significant impact on Indian cinema and has been referred to in several films, including *Om Shanti Om* and, most recently, *Baaghi 2*, where Jacqueline Fernandez tries to recreate the magic of Madhuri. While her outfit (designed by Manish Malhotra) is far skimpier than Madhuri's, it is also more refined. Of course, it is not easy to step into Madhuri's shoes, and the new rendition has not been able to outshine *Tezaab*. The *Hindustan Times* even released a story titled 'People really seem to hate Jacqueline Fernandez's "worst remake ever" of "*Ek Do Teen*"'. Even if the song remains an important point of reference for future films, it will always be the original version, no matter how polarizing the fashion, which will remain iconic.

Chandni

Credited Costume Designers
Kachins, Madhav's Men's Modes, Leena Daru, Bhanu Athaiya, Fitwell, Neeta Lulla and Mischief

This Yash Chopra film with Sridevi and Rishi Kapoor in the lead roles has the rain, the Alps, the roses and of course, lots of chiffon – all the makings of a romantic film. These sweet, delicate and soft accents ensure that the audience cannot help but fall in love with the film and its cast. Rohit, played by Rishi, is a young man from an affluent family who is smitten by just one look with Chandni, played by Sridevi. Chandni comes from a more traditional family and never loses that grounding, instead adapting to her new circumstances. After her initial heartbreak when Rohit leaves due to an accident, she shifts to Mumbai and tries to move on, though she never forgets her first love.

Whether it was her yellow embossed chiffon sari from the song '*Mithwa*' or the white Bharatanatyam-inspired costume she wore in the classical dance scene, Sridevi's styling was kept feminine at all times. It had quite a team working on it, with Bhanu Athaiya, Leena Daru and Neeta Lulla. Leena has been credited with creating the white fitted churidar-kurtas with the coloured chiffon dupatta look, which was copied at stores in Delhi's Chandni Chowk and Mumbai's Dadar Market. Many young women soon wanted to own 'the Chandni Look'.

There is an abundance of white as it was the director's favourite colour. In an interview with film critic Rajeev Masand, conducted for *Vogue India*, Yashji (as he was called in the industry) said, 'I like the colour white as it symbolizes purity. I remember for one classical dance sequence Sridevi was keen to wear the colour peach, but I wanted white; I told the designer to make the same dress in both colours and Sridevi tried both. Even she agreed that the white one gave the whole sequence a pristine look.' Both the white salwar and white sari of the song '*Parbat Se Kaali*' cling to Sridevi as she dances in the rain, but this being a Yash Chopra film, there is only a hint of skin showing, more playful than sensuous. Moreover, since white in films was often only worn by widows, this fashion statement seemed very modern. You can see references to Chandni's style in many later films, such as Karan Johar's *Kuch Kuch Hota Hai*.

1990s & 2000s

1993
Madhuri Dixit

Khalnayak

Credited Costume Designers
**Madhav's Men's Modes, Kachins, Leena Daru, Anja San,
Neeta Lulla and Anna Singh**

Madhuri Dixit's role as Ganga, an undercover policewoman trying to arrest a gangster, Ballu (Sanjay Dutt), is her boldest to date. Who can forget that tight ghagra and backless blouse she wore in the song *'Choli Ke Peeche Kya Hai'*? Translated as 'What is behind the blouse?' this song was considered risqué when it was released, and was even banned on the Indian public television station, Doordarshan. Everything about this song speaks of a woman's sexuality: the sensuous dance moves, the suggestive lyrics and the clothes by renowned costume designer Anna Singh.

Anna recalls that all pieces were bought in from Gujarat to keep the look authentic. A tight fitting, low-waisted and backless blouse became the highlights of the ensemble. The dupatta was worn on the crown of Madhuri's head. Her lip colour was strong and her eyes heavily lined, and there was plenty of rouge – but then she *was* pretending to be a woman of the streets. There was lots of accessorizing, with a full arm of bangles, tribal jewellery and tribal face tattoos.

Perhaps the fact that the character of Ganga was an undercover cop only masquerading as a dancer was a useful plot device at the time, making it more acceptable for Madhuri to be so sexually overt in the movie. There was no need for a guest actress to make an appearance for an item number, as the lead actress provided us with that.

1994
Manisha Koirala

1942: A Love Story

Credited Costume Designer
Bhanu Athaiya

Directed by Vidhu Vinod Chopra, this film is about the freedom struggle and therefore had a strong patriotic message. Naren Singh (Anil Kapoor) is the good-looking son of a wealthy British sympathizer and falls in love with the young and beautiful Rajeshwari 'Rajjo' Pathak (Manisha Koirala), who is the daughter of a well-respected freedom fighter. Manisha was not the first choice for this film, and it was reported by the *Times of India* that Javed Akhtar even wrote the lyrics of '*Ek Ladki Ko Dekha To Aisa Laga*' with Madhuri Dixit in mind. Nonetheless, Manisha played this feminine but feisty character with aplomb. Since the role involved a kissing scene, it was considered a bold move for Manisha, who was still a 'newbie' in the industry, to take on this role. It acted as an indicator that she was not afraid to take on roles that pushed the envelope.

For Naren, it is love at first sight and this is made obvious when he sings '*Ek Ladki Ko Dekha…*' to Rajjo, now an iconic lyrical ode. For this song she wears a simple white cotton salwar, kurta and dupatta; her long hair is in natural curls, and red and white bangles add to a graceful look. The art direction of this film had a true feel for beauty, from the sets to the costumes.

While Manisha's look was authentic to pre-Independence India, it is also a timeless choice, having an appeal that is relevant today. In 2017, Manisha Koirala made a video for the digital channel Unblushed called '78 girls', wherein she revisits the 78 women she has played on screen. For Rajjo, it is this outfit that was recreated. Vidhu Vinod Chopra also recently produced the movie *Ek Ladki Ko Dehka Toh Aisa Laga*, with Anil Kapoor and his daughter, Sonam, part of the project. This influential song was recreated for the film.

1994
Madhuri Dixit

Hum Aapke Hain Koun..!

Credited Costume Designers

Mani Rabadi, Anna Singh, Shabina Khan, Anja San, Neeta Lulla, Ashoo Sharma, Madhav's Men's Modes, Uday Tailors, Bipin Tanna, Sabiha Designs and Allan Gill

This is a Rajshri Productions film at its very best: a wholesome love story that is full of song and dance numbers. Even today, this film, which may seem like an extra-long wedding video, is considered to be one of Indian cinema's most watched films. It won many awards and became one of Bollywood's highest-grossing films at the time. India's sweetheart, Madhuri Dixit, played the female lead, Nisha, who falls in love with Prem, played by one of Bollywood's most favourite actors, Salman Khan.

This Sooraj Barjatya film is a true classic, as is the royal purple sari that was worn by Madhuri in the song '*Didi Tera Devar Deewana*'; in the film, when Prem is mocking Nisha, he also wears a version of this sari. It outshone every other outfit in the film and was designed by Anna Singh, who, thanks to this look, became a household name. There were several designers working on the film, but this sari ensured that, when it came to fashion, Anna was its star. Its rich colour, fabric and gold embroidery, as well as the many bangles and gold jewellery, ensured it caught the eye. The backless blouse and the snug draping of the *pallu* accentuated Madhuri's figure.

A mini version was later made to fit a Barbie doll, as many young girls of the time wanted to wear this sari when they grew up. It became a part of many brides' trousseau for most of that decade, and even today you will see this shot of Madhuri in this outfit in tailoring shops around India. It is a true example of how fashion in film can be a game-changer when it comes to how women dress in India.

1994
Shilpa Shetty

Main Khiladi Tu Anari

Credited Costume Designers
Rocky S., Anja San, Madhav's Men's Modes and Attire

This is the film where it became clear that Shilpa Shetty (who had a double role in this film as Mona, a cabaret dancer, and Basanti, a local village belle) was a girl who loved her fashion. Mona has witnessed the murder of a police inspector by a gangster and drug dealer, Goli (Shakti Kapoor). She agrees to help the police and testify against Goli. Meanwhile, Inspector Karan (Akshay Kumar) is in charge of her safety. Somehow, a young actor, Deepak Kumar (Saif Ali Khan), also becomes entangled in the story and meets Basanti, and they persuade her to be part of their plot to track down and have Goli incriminated.

While Shilpa came out as Bollywood's new glam girl in this film, ironically, this period of cinema is mostly known for its bad fashion. 'We at the time thought we were the cat's whiskers when we wore those clothes [but] in retrospect, we cringe', says Shilpa. However, the short red leopard-print crop top and skirt that she wore in the song '*Chura Ke Dil Mera*' became a rage at that time. Leopard print is a pattern that comes back to fashion every few years, and in the mid-1990s, it was having a real moment.

Though the scene was shot in the heat of Mauritius, this on-trend outfit was still teamed with boots. 'Nothing about this look was planned. It just happened', recalls Shilpa. 'We did not have stylists then, but if you were a big star, you probably worked with a designer. I was not one yet and was only a film old. I was assigned fashion designer Rocky S. (who later became my best friend), who was working on Akshay's costumes. We went shopping and Rocky said, "Let's do sequined boots for the shine and a sequined playsuit." I always loved leopard print and when I reached Mauritius, Sarojji (Saroj Khan), the choreographer, thought the top was too long, cut it with scissors and told me to tie it up. And that's the fashion story!' The look of this song speaks to the kind of filmmaking of the time, where departments were not specialized and everything was a team effort.

1994
Raveena Tandon

Mohra

Credited Costume Designers
**Rocky S., Mischief, Extreme, Workshop, Badasaab,
Madhav's Men's Modes and Bipin Tanna**

In this film, Raveena plays Roma, a journalist, who decides to help Vishal (Sunil Shetty), a man who is imprisoned for murdering the men who raped and killed his sister. Akshay Kumar plays the role of Police Inspector Amar Saxena. But the most defining scene in this star-studded film is the song 'Tip Tip Barsa Pani', which gave Raveena her famous wet-sari moment. In an article titled 'The Hottest Rain Song Ever', *Open Magazine* said of this song, 'It was like winning a lottery, a 5-minute, 50-second joyride for your hormones.'

In a yellow chiffon sari with short frilled sleeves, a large stack of matching yellow bangles on her wrists and gold *payals* on her feet, Roma (Raveena) tries to dance her way into Amar's (Akshay Kumar) heart. The costume designer was Rocky S., who was working with Raveena for the first time and has since worked with her on several projects. He says, 'Being a rain song, things get really transparent, so [the sari] had to be thickly lined, and we made six replicas of it as the fabric was chiffon; [the sari] kept shrinking. This turned Raveena into an instant sex symbol.' This was the first film Raveena and Akshay worked on together, and the two became an off-screen couple.

It took five days to shoot, and despite running a fever, Raveena kept filming till the director, Rajiv Rai, was happy with the song. She recently performed this song again on the finale of Sony TV's reality television show, *Sabse Bada Kalakar*, wearing a yellow sari with a full-length, bell-sleeved blouse, and it was still just as sensual as the original. Judge and actor Ranbir Kapoor gave Raveena a standing ovation. It seems that even more than two decades later, 'Tip Tip Barsa Pani' still manages to thrill people. Certainly, in the mid-1990s, whether it was in *Mohra* or 'Shehar Ki Ladki' from the 1996 film *Rakshak*, Raveena Tandon was Indian cinema's biggest glam girl.

1995
Kajol

Dilwale Dulhania Le Jayenge

Credited Costume Designers

Pamela Chopra, Manish Malhotra, Masculine, Madhav's Men's Modes, Anja San, Prachin's and Karan Johar (for Shah Rukh Khan)

This cult classic marked Aditya Chopra's directorial debut and is Indian cinema's longest-running film. While the director took interest in every aspect of the film, Manish Malhotra was the costume designer of the film, and took full charge of Kajol's look. Karan Johar (an assistant director with a supporting role) was particularly involved with the costumes of Shah Rukh Khan, who plays a rich London boy, Raj Malhotra. Recalls Manish, 'Karan was very interested in clothes and we worked like one team. We were all in the first phases of our careers and we had such a passion for everything – from clothes to cinema.'

Though Kajol was not known to have a keen interest in fashion, in her role as the conservatively-brought up, London-raised Simran, her looks started trending – in particular, the parrot-green lehenga that she wore in the song 'Mehndi Laga Ke Rakhna' that takes place during her sangeet ceremony. It was a modest outfit, with full sleeves and gold details, and has since become an iconic representation of one of Indian cinema's best-loved films. The outfit had made Aditya Chopra nervous because of its unconventional colour, but Manish wanted to use a hue that was not normally seen on screen. Explains Manish, 'Somehow I can understand the colour that will or will not glow on someone's skin. But we've used it very cleverly. It's all bright green because if I had combined that loud colour [with another] then the outfit would have become very loud. So we mixed it only with gold. Also she is sitting throughout the song and she's not really dancing, and not doing very heavy steps tones down the colour.'

The whole silhouette of the outfit seems traditional; this represents the take a young, middle-class, London-bred woman would have on Indian fashion and speaks of the nostalgic view Non-Resident Indians had of Indian fashion in the 1990s. It was indeed a total contrast to her look in the first half of the film, where she's dressed in Western separates, including a blue evening halter gown with a thigh-high slit. Says Manish, 'I feel, because she was a girl from London, she would go and wear a colour that not everybody would. Because girls coming from abroad sometimes have a very interesting take on clothes.'

1995
Urmila Matondkar

Rangeela

Credited Costume Designers
Manish Malhotra (for Urmila Matondkar), Anna Singh (for Jackie Shroff) and Sreenivas Chandra

Costume designer Manish Malhotra has called this film his 'turning point'. This Raj Gopal Verma production helped Urmila Matondkar transform from a child actor to a leading lady. In this romantic comedy, a classic love triangle, she played Mili, a movie extra with aspirations to be more; her best friend is Munna, played by Aamir Khan, a street thug who has romantic feelings for Mili. Actor Raj Kamal, played by Jackie Shroff, helps Mili land an audition for a leading role in an upcoming film called *Rangeela*.

In many ways, this movie marked a new approach to how costumes were viewed in Indian cinema. It was arguably this movie that made Filmfare realize that clothing in films also deserved their attention; Manish Malhotra was the first recipient for the Filmfare Award for Best Costume Designer for his work in *Rangeela*. Says Manish, 'Costumes are not just fashion – they're narratives of the character. There could be a non-fashionable character, a person who is not interested in clothes. So costumes in films are not necessarily fashion. Costume design is about giving a certain look to the character.' He designed Urmila's clothes to be a balance of 'sweet' and 'sensual', using bold prints and lots of colour. Manish says, 'Because at that time there were not that many ready-made clothes available… sourcing was not really possible. You could only source a few things. And I strongly believe that Western clothing needs to be sourced; you can't really make everything.'

Urmila wore knotted crop tops, high-waisted shorts and gilets; this was as fashion-forward as the 1990s ever got. Many oversized T-shirts were also used and converted into dresses. Famously, this is one of the outfits that Urmila wore in the film's most memorable song, '*Tanha Tanha Yahan Pe Jeena*'. Despite multiple outfit changes in the song, however, the one that stands out is the bold red-and-white printed ensemble – an off-the-shoulder crop top with bell sleeves worn over a low-waisted long skirt, featuring many slits. It is fresh and innocent, yet glamorous and alluring. The make-up may now seem a little overdone with the brown and pink eye shadow palette, but that was the look of that time. Urmila became an instant pin-up girl after this film.

1996

Karisma Kapoor

Raja Hindustani

Credited Costume Designers
**Masculine, Jewel and Manish Malhotra
(for Karisma Kapoor and Archana Puran Singh)**

The film made everyone look at Karisma Kapoor in a different light because, until then, she had been known for only her acting skills and not her fashion sense. Karisma played Aarti Sehgal, a big-city heiress who falls in love with Raja, a taxi driver, played by Aamir Khan. For this film, she had long straight hair and subtle make-up, and her clothes had a feel of sophistication. This is considered to be her 'makeover film', and behind this look was Manish Malhotra, who credits its director, Dharmesh Darshan, for insisting that Karisma change her look for this project.

Manish says, 'We kind of toned down Karisma. We were very influenced by the 70s and 60s. I changed her curly hair to straight hair. With her eyes, I was very keen that she wear brown lenses. And I remember when we went to try these lenses, her eyes were watering, and Babitaji (Karisma's mother) said, "She won't be able to wear it", and I told Lolo (Karisma) that it's looking so good on you that you'll never face a camera without it!'

Although in the movie she wears saris and fitted churidar-kurtas that did seem inspired by the 1965 film *Waqt*, it was the short red dress that she wore with a choker that caught everyone's eye. It hugged Karisma's lean figure, showed off her toned legs, and projected her as a glamour girl. You can imagine Parveen Babi or Zeenat Aman wearing this look. This was a turn-around from Karisma's debut film, *Prem Qaidi*, in which she had permed hair, bushy eyebrows and frosty, pink-toned make-up.

1997
Kamal Haasan

Chachi 420

Credited Costume Designers
**Shabina Khan, Simple Kapadia (for Tabu)
and Sulakshana (for songs)**

This Bollywood film's script is an adapted version of the 1993 Hollywood comedy, *Mrs. Doubtfire*. It had Kamal Haasan playing the Robin Williams-inspired role of Jaiprakash, the divorcee who dresses up as a 60-year-old nanny, Lakshmi Godbole, to gain access to his daughter on a daily basis. He managed this metamorphosis with conviction.

For this transformation, Kamal wore a nine-yard Nauvari Maharashtrian sari. Shabina Khan, the costume designer, recalls that the Nauvari sari was chosen because Lakshmi was a very active character, and so it seemed the most appropriate. Shabina, who worked with the late Simple Kapadia on the costumes for this film, adds, 'I remember it would take Kamal four hours in make-up to transform into Lakshmi'. Kamal, who was also the film's director, was particular about his look in the film, she recalls. 'He was so careful that after the prosthetic make-up process had finished, he would only drink water through a straw, so as to not crack the make-up. And he could not eat any solid food', says Shabina. Kamal's saris were bright in colour, and his hair arranged in a low bun adorned with a mogra *gajra*; a big red bindi and slim gold bangles on his wrist finished the look. Wearing foam breasts, he made the most believable 'Chachi'. Kamal's *desi* Mrs. Doubtfire is still considered one of the actor's best performances.

Madhuri Dixit

Dil To Pagal Hai

Credited Costume Designers

**Manish Malhotra (for Madhuri Dixit and Karisma Kapoor),
Karan Johar (for Shah Rukh Khan), Anja San, Kashmira,
Rocky S., Saman Khan and Masculine**

In this film, Pooja and Nisha (Madhuri Dixit and Karisma Kapoor) are dancers, and both are in love with Rahul (Shah Rukh Khan), an accomplished director of a song and dance company. Nisha is Rahul's best friend, and when she is injured during the rehearsal for a play, she is replaced by Pooja, who immediately catches the attention of Rahul even though she is already engaged.

Interestingly, it was the simple cotton salwar kameezes worn by Madhuri that had a ripple effect on fashion, and not the shorts and crop tops of Karisma. This is perhaps because Madhuri's traditional yet contemporary-looking outfits had a soft romantic feel, and you could not help but want her to be the one to win Rahul's heart. Behind the costumes was Manish Malhotra; its director Yash Chopra was also quite particular about how the film was styled.

Manish showed the director 54 dresses before the simple salwar kameez became Madhuri's signature look. She looked fresh and young, yet timeless; this was considered to be a 'Yash Chopra makeover', softening her look from many of her earlier films. In one of Yash Chopra's last interviews, he said to film critic Rajeev Masand, who interviewed him for *Vogue India*, 'I've never believed in approving sketches or dresses on a hanger. I have to see it on the heroine. We spent so much time and money on that process, but I did not know any other way.' Manish kept most of the kurtas sleeveless and the waist section of the kurta unlined, so that it had a sensuous feel. Of course, there was lots of white – one of Yash Chopra's favourite colours.

1997
Urmila Matondkar and Sridevi

Judaai

Credited Costume Designers

Sunita Kapoor, Manish Malhotra, Prachin's, Madhav's Men's Modes, Arjun Khanna and Gabbana

In this love triangle, Kajal (Sridevi), the wife of hard-working Raj (Anil Kapoor), encourages him to divorce her and marry Janhvi (Urmila Matondkar), the daughter of his wealthy boss, so that they can all have a better lifestyle. A film with two glamorous leading women can be problematic for a costume designer, but Manish Malhotra, who worked on the film, says, 'I had worked closely with both before. The actresses saw my honesty and sincerity and they wanted to work with me. I can say we had no issues.'

Manish was there for the shooting of the film in its entirety, including all overseas shoots. He recalls that it was a landmark film for him: 'I'll never forget the outdoor shoot for "Pyaar Pyaar Karte Karte" in Las Vegas.' He adds, 'I started the trend of going abroad to shop; since we were in America, I said, why not do the shopping here? I had no assistants, so I did it all myself. I would take Urmila one day and Sridevi the next day. In the song "Pyaar Pyaar Karte Karte", both wear Western outfits; however, they have a very different look in the rest of the film. And the black ensembles of this song are a stark contrast and so they stood out.' Says producer Boney Kapoor, 'I am sure this was a first in Indian cinema, and also the first time a designer [has ever] shopped abroad for the costumes.'

Sridevi's character starts off as a middle-class wife and wears traditional, fairly simple clothes; after the divorce, as she comes into money, her look becomes garish and ostentatious. Urmila's character turns from a modern, 'Western'-looking young woman into a typical middle-class, simple yet chic, Indian wife. She looks young, in love and desperate for reciprocation, while Sridevi's new avatar comes across like her clothes: bold, loud and over the top. As such, seeing both of them in the complementary Western black ensembles makes 'Pyaar Pyaar Karte Karte' stand out.

1998
Malaika Arora

Dil Se..

Credited Costume Designers
**Pia Benegal, Manish Malhotra, Shabina Khan,
V. Sai and Vaishali Pechauri**

In this Mani Ratnam classic, Amarkant Varma (Shah Rukh Khan) is a journalist who falls in love with Meghna (Manisha Koirala). Amarkant is mesmerized by her but is unaware of the terrible secret she is hiding – that she is a terrorist plotting a suicide attack. The movie was a critical success and has A.R. Rahman's stellar music (he won Best Music Director for this film at the Filmfare Awards), but the true star of the film was the song *'Chaiyya Chaiyya'*, in which Malaika Arora dances on top of a moving train with Shah Rukh. This song marked Malaika's debut as an item girl. Until then, Malaika was primarily known for being a model and TV show host, so seeing her in an Indian ghagra and choli was unexpected. The scene was shot in Tamil Nadu's Ooty but there is nothing South Indian about the way Malaika is dressed.

Manish Malhotra, who designed Malaika's costume, admits that it is the work of Bhanu Athaiya – known for her village belle looks in the films of the 1970s – that he referred to. 'I'm always inspired by Bhanuji's work and, yes, that was in my mind', explains Manish. Hence, if the clothes are reminiscent of Rekha in the 1979 film *Mr. Natwarlal*, it is no coincidence. Malaika's outfit also has a feel of the black and red costumes of Rajasthan's Kalbelia dancers. *Maang tikas*, armlets and bangles are all part of the Kalbelia dancer dress.

As for dancing on top of a moving train, recalls Malaika, 'It was scary as hell. Because I kept thinking I was going to fall off, as the jewellery was very heavy.' Of course, she had nothing to worry about, as Manish had everything under control: 'That's the trick of costumes; we know how to use the fabric and place embroidery so that it looks elaborate but it's still dance-friendly.' While the film did not do as well as expected commercially, the song *'Chaiyya Chaiyya'* ushered in a new age for Malaika, who has since appeared in several films as an item girl.

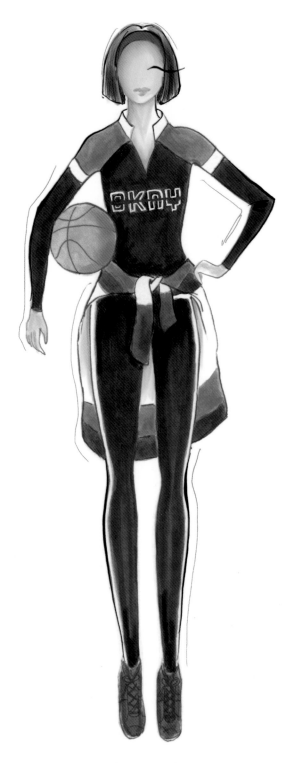

1998
Kajol

Kuch Kuch Hota Hai

Credited Costume Designers
**Manish Malhotra, Shabina Khan (for Shah Rukh Khan,
Anupam Kher, Johny Lever) and Bipin Tanna (for dancers)**

Karan Johar's directorial debut, this film was about a love triangle that begins in college. Playing the popular boy is Shah Rukh Khan as Rahul, and his tomboy best friend is Kajol as Anjali, who secretly has feelings for him. Rahul, though, is infatuated with Tina, played by Rani Mukerji, the feminine daughter of the college principal. Though Tina marries Rahul, she dies after giving birth to their daughter, also named Anjali.

Kajol's character, in the first half of the film, has short hair and wears a broad hairband. For Manish Malhotra, hair has always been a focal point in his films. This is why he was sure that Kajol's hair needed to be cut short, to go with the tomboy she was portraying. Although it looked like everything was bought from branded stores, the clothes were actually tailored to give Kajol that casual vibe. 'I would pick up a lot of clothes, but I altered the backs, added zips to the T-shirts, cut the T-shirts open… And there were lots of T-shirts that I stitched. Because when you buy ready-made clothes, it's not like they fit really well.'

You could say that Manish and Karan were the first to bring the sporty-chic look to film in India before the country became more global in its outlook. The sporty look was coupled with the use of logo T-shirts and sweatshirts from brands such as DKNY and Tommy Hilfiger, and changed teenagers' outlook on fashion. This film came out six years before Tommy Hilfiger, one of the most famous international fashion labels, came to India, but thanks to this film it was already one of the best-known brands in the country without having paid a penny for product placement.

You eventually see Kajol's character transform from a dungarees and tracksuit-wearing teenager to a graceful young woman; in the second half of the film, she becomes a sari-wearing, long-haired, 'conventional' Indian belle. Says film critic Rajeev Masand, 'If there's any film director in Bollywood after Yash Chopra who is known for how he presents his heroines on screen, then it's Karan Johar. In fact, Johar has frequently admitted that his obsession with aesthetics, his attention to costume – particularly the heroine's – came from his abiding love for Yash Chopra's cinema.'

1999
Aishwarya Rai

Hum Dil De Chuke Sanam

Credited Costume Designers
Neeta Lulla, Shabina Khan and Allan Gill (for dancers)

This film sparked the pairing of Salman Khan and Aishwarya Rai, both on and off screen. Directed by Sanjay Leela Bhansali, it is based on the Bengali novel *Na Hanyate* by Maitreyi Devi. Nandini (Aishwarya Rai) is the happy-go-lucky daughter of an important proponent of Indian classical music. It is announced that a man named Sameer (Salman Khan) will be staying with them to study music. The two quickly fall in love, but this union does not go down well with the family, as Nandini is already engaged to Vanraj (Ajay Devgn). Eventually, Vanraj discovers that she loves another man and tries to reunite her with Sameer in Italy.

As the first part of the story is based in Gujarat, with Aishwarya playing the daughter of a leading classical musician, her clothes are quite traditional. Her look in this film became an inspiration for brides-to-be and for festive occasions. With costumes designed by Neeta Lulla, Aishwarya's clothes are conventionally feminine with a hint of the contemporary. The song '*Chand Chupa Badal Mein*' talks about the meaning of Karva Chauth; for this moonlit number, Aishwarya wore a lavender lehenga, sprinkled with silver embroidery. From the colour to the shimmer, it worked perfectly with the mood and highlighted her eyes. The lavender colour was a measured choice.

Says Neeta, 'From the onset, having read the script and about Nandini's background and character, that she was a highly educated girl living in a conservative Gujarati family, my thought process went towards the use of unusual hues and away from the typical Indian jewel tones. Plus, I didn't want to steer the attention away from Aishwarya's face and expressions… [the outfits] complemented the background of the night skies.' Extensions were added to Aishwarya's hair to ensure her face was perfectly framed, and the lehenga was hand-embroidered in Neeta's studio to ensure the piece had just the correct amount of shimmer. This lavender outfit became part of one of the film's most beautiful moments.

2001

Kareena Kapoor

Asoka

Credited Costume Designers
**Anu Vardhan, Manish Malhotra (for Kareena Kapoor)
and Naresh Rohira (for Shah Rukh Khan)**

This is an epic historical drama, and though it is based on the early life of Emperor Asoka, it is more fiction than fact. Asoka (Shah Rukh Khan) is a prince who has been asked to leave the kingdom by his mother after a family dispute. He then meets Kaurwaki (Kareena Kapoor), a beautiful runaway princess whom he falls in love with and later marries. This film came early in Kareena's career and was an indicator that she was not afraid to take on roles some people may consider bold.

In the song 'San Sanana', she wore a bandeau-style blouse teamed with a dhoti-style skirt; there was a sensual feel to everything she wore. It does seem like her outfits are inspired by those from another film based on ancient India – Amrapali, the 1966 classic that had Vyjayanthimala in the lead. 'Asoka was very difficult in terms of construction. It referenced Amrapali in a way, but it is also very different from Amrapali. Because in Amrapali, Vyjayanthimala's character is very graceful. But in Kareena's case, she's very rustic', says the film's costume designer, Manish Malhotra.

This is why the director, Santosh Sivan, asked Manish to use textured fabrics such as jute for the costumes and to incorporate tribal tattoos in the make-up. 'In Amrapali, the fabrics are very soft. But here the director… did not want that softness', says Manish. He explains that this film, as far as costumes go, proved to be challenging as jute is not an easy fabric to work with. Ultimately, Kareena's outfits, coupled with her flawless skin and kohl-rimmed eyes, made you take notice, enchanting audiences right from the first trailer of the movie.

2001
Preity Zinta

Dil Chahta Hai

Credited Costume Designer
Arjun Bhasin

A film about the coming of age of three young men, it also spoke about the coming of age of Indian cinema. Farhan Akhtar's *Dil Chahta Hai* brought a new cool to Bollywood; all the clothes in the film seem like they slipped out of the wardrobe of a real twenty-something living in Mumbai's Bandra. The characters include Akash (Aamir Khan), Sameer (Saif Ali Khan) and Siddharth, a.k.a. 'Sid' (Akshaye Khanna). The women they fall for are Shalini (Preity Zinta), Pooja (Sonali Kulkarni) and the older divorcee, Tara (Dimple Kapadia). It was not only the directorial debut of Farhan Akhtar, but also the first film that costume designer and stylist Arjun Bhasin worked on. Having studied at New York University's film school and worked on projects in America, Arjun related more to Hollywood than Bollywood. It was his fresh eye that helped make *Dil Chahta Hai* the cult film it is today.

Preity Zinta's vivacious wardrobe was one that seemed to delight many college-going women at the time. In the movie, when Shalini and Akash go to the Sydney Opera House, she wears a strapless, form-fitting dress, with drop earrings and lines of beaded necklaces draped over one shoulder, and her hair is curled and worn in a natural half-updo. This effortless look stood out, as onscreen female characters who came from affluent families were usually seen with perfectly coiffed hair. The hairstyles of the characters, by the famed Adhuna Bhabani Akhtar, became all the rage at the time.

As international as this look is, Arjun recounts that the outfit was made by a tailor. There were very few international brands available in India at the time, and as this was Akhtar's first film, there were no budgets for shopping trips abroad. The necklace was made by Arjun's sister, Niharika Bhasin Khan. Keeping things real is what Arjun concentrated on, and this is why so many urban Indians, including those from upper-class families who might have looked down on 'filmi' fashion, turned to *Dil Chahta Hai* for style. Arjun did not offer a new look per scene, which was the norm back then in mainstream Indian cinema. Instead, he often reused clothes and accessories in the film to make the dressing seem 'everyday'. *Dil Chahta Hai* has become a textbook example of how costume can play an important part in crafting a movie.

2001
Kareena Kapoor

Kabhi Khushi Kabhie Gham...

Credited Costume Designers
**Manish Malhotra, Shabina Khan (for Shah Rukh Khan)
and Rocky S. (for Hrithik Roshan)**

This Karan Johar film was promoted with the tagline, 'It's all about loving your parents.' The plot involves a patriarchal father who disowns his adopted son for marrying beneath them, a younger brother who leaves to find the disowned brother, an emotional mother, a doting wife and her younger sister. The story travels from Delhi to London and back. It is a family drama that is meant to tug at your heartstrings and had all the cinema heavyweights of that time – Amitabh Bachchan, Shah Rukh Khan, Hrithik Roshan, Jaya Bachchan, Kajol and Kareena Kapoor.

The clothes of the younger sister, Pooja (Kareena Kapoor), a fashion-obsessed, London-based university student, became the centre of everyone's attention. Her looks included crop tops (which became her signature style in the movie), often with very low backs – she's seen pairing them with bell-bottoms, short skirts and even a *sharara*. It was the perfect combination of cloth (or the lack of it) and character. She was the fun, glam girl in this otherwise tear-jerker of a film. Recalls Manish Malhotra, who crafted the costumes of this film, 'In the early 90s, when there was a lot of NRI [Non-Resident Indian] exposure to Indian films, the youth were completely confused between orthodox parents at home and a different culture outside… It kind of made all those films we did – if you remember Kareena in "Bole Chudiyan" with the *sharara*, which had an asymmetrical top.'

His work, which mixed contemporary Indian fashion with Western elements, had an immediate connection with Indian women who had been born and brought up in the West. The pink outfit Kareena wore in '*Bole Chudiyan*' went on to become the ensemble every young woman wanted to wear to her best friend's sangeet, especially if you were an NRI. The song honours the traditional Punjabi festival of Karva Chauth, where ladies are usually dressed in red and gold; in '*Bole Chudiyan*', however, the modern silver-embellished, rose-pink *sharara* that Pooja wears adds a 'hip' feel to this Indian custom.

2001
Karisma Kapoor

Zubeidaa

Credited Costume Designer
Pia Benegal

This film, directed by Shyam Benegal, is based on the life of Zubeida (spelled 'Zubeidaa' in the film), a spirited actress, portrayed by Karisma Kapoor. Zubeidaa's father does not approve of her career choice and arranges her marriage, which ends in a divorce and leaves her as a single mother. She later becomes the second wife of Maharaja Vijayendra Singh of Fatehpur, played by Manoj Bajpayee. Its scriptwriter was Khalid Mohammed, the son of Zubeida Begum Dhanrajgir, and featured a cast that included Rekha, Lillete Dubey and Rajit Kapur. This film was a successful combination of commercial and artistic cinema.

Behind the fashion was Shyam's daughter, Pia Benegal, known for her attention to detail. The costumes are regal and resplendent – from the colourful saris Zubeidaa wears for polo matches to the delicate ivory salwar kameez with gold detailing she wears in the song, 'Mehndi Hai Rachnewali'. However, it is the outfit that she wears in the festival scene, where she sits with Maharani Mandira Devi, played by Rekha, that inspired many brides-to-be at that time. In the red and gold *paushak* that had green highlights and a matching *odhini*, Karisma looks truly splendid. The magnificent jewellery, which included a *rakhdi* (head ornament) and layered *kundan* necklaces, added a regal touch.

As scriptwriter Khalid recalls, 'I showed the collection of photographs, shot at photo studios, of my mother. She was fond of photo shoots, evidently; some of the portraits were candid, others were elaborate, showing her in chiffon saris and a pearl necklace, as well as the royal *jadau* jewellery of Jodhpur… The portraits showed her in various permed hairstyles, rich lehengas and saris. Again, naturally, I hoped these would be replicated in the film. But how could they be? They would have looked far too ostentatious, and wouldn't have gone with the spirit of the film as directed by Shyam Benegal. He dignified the screenplay majorly, replacing the ostentation of the 1950s with elegance and grace relevant to a biopic made in 2001. And the entire credit for the colour palettes, jewellery and accessories goes to Shyam Sir's daughter, Pia Benegal, who is an outstanding designer.'

2002
Aishwarya Rai and Madhuri Dixit

Devdas

Credited Costume Designers
Abu Jani–Sandeep Khosla, Neeta Lulla and Reza Shariffi

This Sanjay Leela Bhansali film is adapted from the classic Bengali novel *Devdas*, written by Sarat Chandra Chattopadhyay. It tells the story of a young man, Devdas (Shah Rukh Khan), who has just returned to India after studying in England for a decade. Devdas is in love with his childhood friend, Paro (Aishwarya Rai); however, his family does not agree to the union and she is married off to another man by her family. A grief-stricken Devdas then turns to a life of alcoholism and finds comfort in the arms of a courtesan named Chandramukhi (Madhuri Dixit).

The most highlighted moment of *Devdas* is the song *'Dola Re Dola'*, as it puts together two of Indian cinema's most beautiful women, Aishwarya Rai and Madhuri Dixit. Both are trained in classical dance, and this song was almost like a dance-off between them. Both wore Bengali-style saris, with Neeta Lulla and Abu Jani–Sandeep Khosla working closely on these looks. Although both were in the traditional colours of white and red and looked similar, the outfits were designed keeping in mind the body types and requirements of the women.

Says Neeta, 'I worked on a 15-yard sari drape for Aishwarya to add girth to the skirt area so that when she moved, the sari moved in a *gher*-like form. The lehenga and Madhuri's drape were structured and then made by her designers [Abu Jani and Sandeep Khosla] into a 12-yard drape to complement her figure and give her the movement desired for the song'. Aishwarya's sari and motifs depicted delicacy, whereas Madhuri's had a stronger feel. It took craftsmen six months to make each of these pieces and each one was pre-draped by Neeta personally. It was finished with traditional gold and *kundan* pieces of jewellery that were so heavy, they caused Aishwarya's ears to bleed during the shoot. As to who 'won' the dance off, it turned out to be a draw. Both looked beautiful, and both danced with complete grace.

2002
Madhuri Dixit

Devdas

Credited Costume Designers
Neeta Lulla, Abu Jani–Sandeep Khosla and Reza Shariffi

This marks the third time a film has been made based on Sarat Chandra Chattopadhyay's novel, *Devdas*. As the first one in colour, and directed by Sanjay Leela Bhansali, fashion-wise it is this version of *Devdas* that is the most important. Abu Jani, Sandeep Khosla, Neeta Lulla and Reza Shariffi all received a National Film Award for Best Costume Design for their work on the film. Abu Jani and Sandeep Khosla oversaw the clothes for three main characters, Chandramukhi (Madhuri Dixit), Devdas (Shah Rukh Khan) and Chunnilal (Jackie Shroff), but for this duo it was Madhuri's character that held the most interest. Abu and Sandeep say, 'She is dressed in exquisite Benares saris, brocades and silks… [and] kurtas teamed with beautiful transparent dupattas and embroidered blouses, inspired by the 1930s and 1940s.'

The gorgeous mirror-work lehenga worn by Madhuri was part of the 'Fabric of India' exhibition held at the Victoria and Albert Museum in London in 2015. Designed by Abu Jani and Sandeep Khosla, the ghagra is hand-embroidered and features mirrors embedded in the fabric using zardozi embroidery. The flared 10-panel ghagra took a team of highly skilled artisans two months to make and weighs over 10 kilograms as a set. Say the designers, 'Embroideries from Gujarat have always fascinated us, and we work extensively on both thread and mirror-work techniques from the state. We loved reinventing traditional mirror-work, which is quintessentially folksy, into the most fabulous couture.' This ghagra was not actually used in the movie as it was too heavy and did not work with the choreography of the dance it was made for. But it was such a trendsetting piece that the director wanted it to be featured, so it was used in promotional posters. It helped spark an interest in Gujarat's vibrant fashion traditions.

Chandramukhi at her home is always shown in fine mulmul or cotton skirts, with *gota* work and *ghungroos* paired with small embroidered cholis. But as a courtesan, her *jadau* and gold jewellery are plentiful; even with her heavily embellished gold lehenga, she wears many bangles, statement rings, necklaces and earrings. It is one of Indian cinema's most decadent moments, and reflects the fact that *Devdas* was one of the most expensive Indian films made till that date.

2003
Preity Zinta

Kal Ho Naa Ho

Credited Costume Designer
Manish Malhotra

A film written and produced by Karan Johar, *Kal Ho Naa Ho* is a testament to his forte: writing stories based on family and love. For this movie, the backdrop is one of Karan's favourite cities – New York. Preity Zinta plays the young half-Punjabi, half-Caucasian Naina Catherine Kapur, who is a bookworm. Naina falls in love with her charismatic neighbour, Aman Mathur (Shah Rukh Khan). Even though Aman is also in love with her, he tries to get Naina close to her best friend, Rohit Patel (Saif Ali Khan), because Aman is terminally ill.

With Manish Malhotra behind the costumes, everything she wore was very much on-trend for that time, be it the one-shoulder tops or the trench coats, or even her signature accessory: a pair of dark-rimmed glasses, depicting her geeky side. While most of the Western ensembles were sourced from international brands, there is of course one Indian ensemble that is a signature Manish Malhotra outfit. The slim blue lehenga Preity wears for the engagement scene and for the breakout song '*Maahi Ve*', with its nude underlay, became quite the rage at the time. Although the outfit had embellishments in thread work and sequins, Manish did not use any silver or gold. 'We wanted to keep it modern; she was a girl from New York who did not enjoy glamour normally, so we needed to keep it elegant', explains Manish.

The way that Naina goes from Western to Indian clothes had a very real feel about it. Says film critic and author, Udita Jhunjhunwala, 'It captured the modern NRI [Non-Resident Indian] who easily transitions from Western to Indian wear… [though] there is no substitute for Indian garments when it comes to tradition and festivities and the looks in *Kal Ho Naa Ho*.' The testament to this is the fact that clients still ask Manish Malhotra for ensembles inspired by the blue lehenga look.

2004
Rani Mukerji

Hum Tum

Credited Costume Designers
**Mamta Anand and Reza Shariffi (for Saif Ali Khan), Manish Malhotra
(for Rani Mukerji) and Shiraz Siddique (for Jimmy Shergill)**

A love story between two characters that spans years, *Hum Tum* was one of Kunal
Kohli's earliest films – and he was clear that this film needed to be authentic and
'real'. Rani Mukerji played Rhea and Saif Ali Khan played Karan, a cartoonist. The two
meet on a plane from Delhi to New York and end up spending a few hours exploring
Amsterdam during a stopover, after which they part ways. During the course of the
film, Rhea gets married to another man and ends up becoming a young widow. After
many ups and downs, Rhea and Karan end up as a married couple.

Rhea's look at the start of film, when she is fresh out of college, with her short hair
and casual approach to fashion, was one that many young women at that time found
inspiring. Says Kunal, 'The hairstyles were written into the script. It was simple logic;
the film spans many years and we do change our hair and look as time passes. But
I found in many Indian films this was not taken into account.' He also asked Manish
Malhotra, who was behind Rani's costume design, to prepare a wardrobe of clothes
for each period. 'She repeats clothes, as a normal girl. I think she wears the jeans in the
song "*Ladki Kyon*" a few times in the film.' The halter shirt Rani wore for this song, Kunal
recollects, was Manish's idea, as were the colourful sneakers and backpack. 'A person's
whole body language changes with clothes. We shot the song in the morning, and
as soon as Rani put on the sneakers and jeans, she just bounced around. Then, in the
afternoon, we shot the scene after she becomes a widow, and she wears heels and a
skirt and has a shawl around her, and immediately her whole poise changed.'

It was Rani's look from the film that made shorter hair the go-to style for many teenage
girls in India, perhaps because so many could relate to Rhea's character. There was
something fun and unexpected about the voluminous bob; short hair after school age
used to be considered unladylike and rebellious. Rani Mukerji's haircut, however, was
unobtrusive, though still a nudge towards modernity.

2004
Sushmita Sen

Main Hoon Na

Credited Costume Designers

Sanjeev Mulchandani, Karan Johar (for Shah Rukh Khan), Manish Malhotra (for Sushmita Sen) and Navin Shetty (for Sunil Shetty)

Part comedy, part romance and part thriller, this Farah Khan film is set against the volatile relationship of India-Pakistan, and is a proper masala film. Shah Rukh Khan played Ram Prasad Sharma, an army major who becomes an undercover student to protect Sanjana Bakshi, played by Amrita Rao, a general's daughter whose life is under threat from a former paramilitary officer. While Ram is at the college, Chandni, a chemistry teacher played by Sushmita Sen, catches his attention and sparks fly. It is no surprise that he falls for Chandni, with her chiffon saris draped to show off her body.

Costume designer Manish Malhotra says, 'Farah and I had a big 70s influence and wanted to get back to saris. There's something very glamorous about a sari and very attractive… I had a very Zeenat Aman vibe in my mind.' The knotted sari blouses were obviously a nod to Sharmila Tagore and Mumtaz. One sari that stands out is the chiffon polka-dot one, which Chandni wears in the scene where Ram is on his knees, being punished outside the principal's office and he sees her walking towards him. It has a retro vibe, but thanks to the contrasting *pallu*, the modern accessories and hairstyle, it feels au courant.

Attention was paid to every detail, with Farah being very involved in costume and prop choices. For instance, even the files that Chandni carried were chosen with care to ensure they complemented the outfit being worn. Manish says that he used to tease Farah by saying she was more interested in the files than the saris. Nonetheless, thanks to this look, the polka-dot sari came back to the forefront of fashion.

2005
Aishwarya Rai

Bunty Aur Babli

Credited Costume Designers
Aki Narula, Ameira Punvani and Bipin Tanna (for dancers)

Shaad Ali's second film, which was inspired by the American cult classic, *Bonnie and Clyde*, has Aishwarya Rai making a special appearance as a bar girl for the song '*Kajra Re*'. Based on the Qawwali genre of music, this hit track features Aishwarya dressed like a modern-day courtesan in a bright-hued lehenga without a dupatta. The choli is short and has a deep cut-out in the back, and the lehenga is worn low. Her hair is straight and her make-up not overdone, giving the look a contemporary feel. But the *passa*, *payal* and *hath-phool* ensure that it has a traditional side. '*Kajra Re*' also features Abhishek Bachchan, who plays the 'Clyde' character, Rakesh, a.k.a. Bunty, and Amitabh Bachchan as joint commissioner of police, Dashrath Singh. It is said that this sensual number also marked the beginning of Abhishek's relationship with Aishwarya, whom he later married.

Recalls film critic and author, Udita Jhunjhunwala, 'The song became famous for the troika – Amitabh Bachchan, Abhishek Bachchan and Aishwarya Rai – [as well as] Gulzar's lyrics, Shankar-Ehsaan-Loy's music… [and] the colours, styling and choreography. Aishwarya did look smoking hot in that lehenga and short choli. "*Kajra Re*" was a rage in nightclubs and, of course, the audience was curious to see the chemistry between Aishwarya and Abhishek.' There is no question that the vibrant styling of this song added some punch to this item number and ensured that Aishwarya's appearance was indeed special.

The choli from Aishwarya's look in *Bunty Aur Babli* made an appearance in another film, *Band Baaja Baaraat*, where it was worn by a background dancer with another lehenga. Often, production houses keep the costumes after a film and reuse them in some way; both *Bunty Aur Babli* and *Band Baaja Baaraat* come under the Yash Raj banner. Sometimes actors do request to keep the outfit, but clearly, as much as Aishwarya sizzled in this look, she decided to let the production house keep the costume.

2005
Rani Mukerji

Bunty Aur Babli

Credited Costume Designers
Aki Narula, Ameira Punvani and Bipin Tanna (for dancers)

Rani Mukerji is 'Bonnie' in this *Bonnie and Clyde*-inspired film about two small-town con artists who manage to pull off some major scams. Playing Vimmi, a.k.a. Babli, Rani started a whole new fashion trend with her unique look. For this film, director Shaad Ali asked Aki Narula, who as a fashion designer was known to be inspired by street trends, to be the costume designer. He put Babli in bright collared kurtis with matching Patiala salwars and finished the look with a contrasting, vibrantly-hued *jhola* bag. Tailors around India called this look 'the *Bunty Aur Babli* suit'. Aki was able to draw on the way small-town India dressed while giving a very urban and young feel to the film – and it had an instant appeal. It was a modern-day example of how fashion filters down from the big screen to the streets, and vice versa.

While Aki received a lot of good press for his styling, he also was accused of copying designer Suneet Varma for one of the looks. The blue chiffon poncho and black embroidered bootleg trousers worn in the film by Rani was identical to a look from Suneet's Fall/Winter 2003 collection. Aki claimed that his team had sourced the piece from a store in Mumbai, a common practice for costume designers. Eventually, a press conference was held at Lakmé India Fashion Week to try and clarify the matter, and Suneet even filed a case against Aki and the production house. While many may have forgotten about this incident, it proves how influential the reel can be on the Indian fashion industry, often in more powerful ways than expected.

2005
Vidya Balan

Parineeta

Credited Costume Designer
Subarna Ray Chaudhuri

This film marked the debut of Vidya Balan. Although she had appeared on the small screen and in music videos, she had never appeared in a full-length feature film. Adapted from the Bengali novella *Parineeta*, written in 1914 by Sarat Chandra Chattopadhyay, the film was produced by Vidhu Vinod Chopra and directed by Pradeep Sarkar. Vidya played Lalita, who is caught in a love triangle that is set in Kolkata in 1962.

Lalita is always fashionably dressed and wears some beautiful traditional drapes; one of the stand-out pieces is the red and white Baluchari sari in the song '*Kasto Mazza*'. It is impossible to miss the feminine frills on the neckline and the border of the sleeves on the choli in that song. The blouses in the movie were given a lot of attention: in one scene, there is an oversized bejewelled flower at the back, and in another there are puffed sleeves, another typical Bengali detail. Lalita is clearly a woman of good taste, symbolizing that she also has good judgement. Throughout the film her hair is middle-parted, again speaking of tradition. But slightly more daring touches, such as the low back of the blouse, imply that she is also a woman who knows her mind.

The costumes were designed by Subarna Ray Chaudhuri and marked the beginning of Vidya's association with the sari. As Kolkata is the city Subarna is from, this project for her had authenticity. 'My favourite sari is the red and white Benarasi [Vidya] wears, the one that you see in most of the film posters', explains Subarna. She went to Old Calcutta to do most of the sourcing, to markets such as Bara Bazaar, where many of the sari shops are over a hundred years old. 'I asked them to take out old pieces that had been restored', she adds. The red and white Benarasi was found among these; it was made of a silk so light that it clung to the body. 'You do not find Benarasi fabrics made of such fine and pure silk', she says. That piece was more than 60 years old. For some old, restored saris, she had to cut borders and motifs and apply them to new saris to ensure they had a fresh look yet were authentic. She managed to get the small details perfect thanks to her research, which involved meeting friends' aunts, as well as her family members, and seeing their personal collections and pictures from that period.

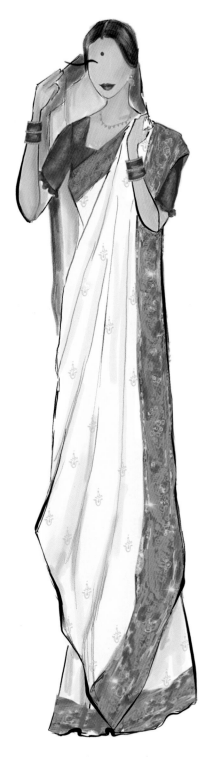

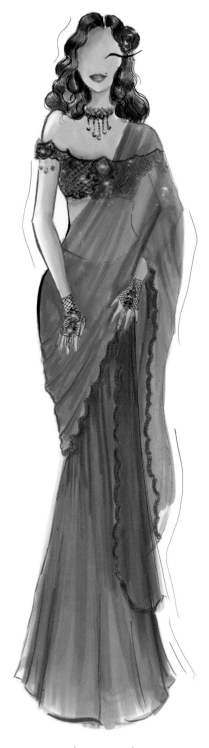

2005
Rekha

Parineeta

Credited Costume Designer
Subarna Ray Chaudhuri

Rekha made a cameo appearance in the film as a nightclub singer, and being the woman she is, she made a strong impact. As far as style goes, Rekha was always a pioneer. She loves to be glamorous, yet always keeps it Indian. She wore a red flamenco-style sari in *Parineeta*, and the costume designer for the film, Subarna Ray Chaudhuri, says, 'The cabaret singers of that time would have worn a gown, but Rekha wanted a sari, so we married the two for this sari-gown.'

Very much inspired by looks from the Moulin Rouge in Paris, the diaphanous drape, black gloves, vamp-red lips and strong eyeliner were meant to make you look at nothing but her. A frill petticoat added volume to the sari, and her blouse seductively fell off one shoulder. This was a costume specifically crafted to enhance her energetic performance for her song *'Kaisi Paheli Zindagaani'*.

There were some who felt the look was a little 'too much', but it was deliberate, and the styling made it obvious that this song was meant to stand out from the rest of film. It also proved that Rekha, at any age, will always command attention.

2006
Bipasha Basu

Corporate

Credited Costume Designers
Shefalina, Rocky S. (for Bipasha Basu) and Gabbana (for Raj Babbar)

Directed by Madhur Bhandarkar, this film changed the way model-turned-actress Bipasha Basu was perceived. Madhur is known for his 'real' films that often have women as protagonists. A movie based on pesticide issues in India, it explores the insider dealing that goes on in many industrialist business families.

Bipasha Basu played Nishigandha Dasgupta, the no-nonsense vice president of a company, who becomes a victim of corporate politics. Recalls Madhur, 'Rocky S. did the clothes for this film. I had a very clear brief – Bipasha till then had been known as a glam girl. The roles she had done before had a very fashionable feel, and I wanted to break this image. I knew she was the right person for this part and could be both strong and fragile. So I told Rocky to keep it very corporate looking; be it the pinstripes or the pulled-back hair, it had to be a clean look.'

The accessories and make-up were kept minimal too, to keep the attention on Bipasha's performance. Madhur says, 'I remember on the first day, when she stepped out of her van, I felt she had too much make-up on and made her make-up artist tone her look down.' The jackets were kept slightly longer as Bipasha had many walking scenes and Madhur felt the length would give some movement to the shots. The professional look of this film became a point of reference for many young female white-collar workers in India at that time.

2006
Aishwarya Rai

Dhoom 2

Credited Costume Designer
Anaita Shroff Adajania

The *Dhoom* series has been one of Yash Raj Films' most successful franchises. This action cop series has two recurring characters: assistant police commissioner Jai Dixit (Abhishek Bachchan) and his sidekick, Ali Khan (Uday Chopra). *Dhoom 2* remains the most sizzling of all the films in the series thanks to the inclusion of Aishwarya Rai. In this second instalment of *Dhoom*, Aishwarya plays Sunehri, whose role was obviously inspired by Catwoman. Sunehri knew she was sexy, and was not scared to show it; Aishwarya, the former Miss India, looked every bit a beauty contest winner in this role with her toned body. At the time of the film's release, every newspaper could only write about one thing – the bikini that Aishwarya wore.

Even today, it is Aishwarya's image in a turquoise-blue swimsuit that you probably recall when you think of the *Dhoom* series. In actuality it was a one piece with a cut-out, and it was layered with a bikini top inside and a short white skirt below it. No one had ever expected that Aishwarya could look hotter than a '*Baywatch* babe' – and it was Anaita Shroff Adajania who made it happen. At the time, Anaita was the fashion director of the leading fashion publication, *L'Officiel India*, had already worked on the original *Dhoom* and had also styled the songs for Karan Johar's hit, *Kal Ho Naa Ho*.

Known for bringing high-end fashion to the silver screen, Anaita sourced this swimsuit from Rio De Janerio (much of the film was shot there), and completed Aishwarya's look with highlighted sun-kissed hair, drop earrings and a cuff. The detailing of this outfit truly shows how the right costume designer can add authenticity to a film. Says Anaita, 'My whole idea with *Dhoom 2* was to use brands very unpredictably as I felt this would create an overall cutting-edge style for the viewer. I remember giving Ash [Aishwarya] a Pucci gown to wear when she's lounging at home. Now, you can't get more fashionably eccentric than that.' And while Bipasha Basu, who was also part of the cast, wore some tiny bikinis, it was Aishwarya in her blue monokini that crafted an image no one could forget.

2006
Rani Mukerji

Kabhi Alvida Naa Kehna

Credited Costume Designers
Manish Malhotra and Anaita Shroff Adajania (for songs)

This is a Karan Johar film, so it comes as no surprise that there is a multi-star cast and that his favourite city, New York, serves as the backdrop. Dev (Shah Rukh Khan), a bitter soccer player whose career has been cut short due to an injury, is married to a successful fashion magazine editor, Rhea (Preity Zinta). The 'other woman' is Maya (Rani Mukerji), who is married to a seemingly perfect husband, Rishi Talwar (Abhishek Bachchan). The film explores the subject of infidelity through a sympathetic lens.

The film is noteworthy for its fashion; Karan Johar worked with Manish Malhotra and Anaita Shroff Adajania to create influential looks. Says leading film critic Rajeev Masand, 'For Rani Mukerji – who had appeared in two films by Karan Johar already but never playing the main heroine in either – landing the female lead in *Kabhi Alvida Naa Kehna* was a big coup… which meant the top designers and stylists working on her look, the best make-up artists, great songs, great costumes and great locations.' In the film, Rani moved from scrumptious sweaters worn under chic coats to sensual chiffon saris, and was even seen in a corset with a whip to spice up her marriage.

For Rajeev, the film's stand-out style moment is '*Tumhi Dekho Naa*', popularly referred to as 'the colour song', with its chiffon saris and modern, small cholis. Karan had wanted to make a larger-than-life love song and came up with an innovative concept: they would shoot different portions of the song with a different, bold colour each. Not just the actor and actresses' costumes, but the entire frame would have a colour palette, starting with blue, then black, autumnal orange, bright pink, red and finally, green.

In its time, *Kabhi Alvida Naa Kehna* dictated fashion trends. With its use of brands such as Louis Vuitton and Christian Dior, which had just entered the country, it showed urban Indians how designer accessories could become an essential part of their wardrobe. Rani, with her 'non-fashion' image, made the perfect muse for these brands as she did not intimidate audiences, who could then relate to her – and her use of high-end accessories.

2006
Bipasha Basu

Omkara

Credited Costume Designers
**Dolly Ahluwalia Tiwari, Rocky S. (for Bipasha Basu)
and Anna Singh (for Ajay Devgn)**

The director Vishal Bhardwaj is an evident admirer of William Shakespeare, having made three films based on the English playwright's work. In *Omkara*, Vishal manages to stay true to the story of *Othello*, but gives it a 21st-century Bollywood do-over. Winning multiple awards in India, including Filmfare's Best Costume Designer for Dolly Ahluwalia Tiwari, the film was screened at both the Cannes International Film Festival and Cairo International Film Festival.

Ajay Devgn played the title role, a bandit boss who has the backing of local politicians. The Bianca of the film is Billo, played by Bipasha Basu; the role of a dancer-girl and mistress gives her one of her all-time career highs with the song *'Beedi'*. It is almost the film's item song, but only unofficially, as it is performed by one of the main cast members. From its music, composed by Vishal himself, to its lyrics, written by Gulzar, to Bipasha's fresh take on the nautch (dance) girl, dancing with steps choreographed by Ganesh Archarya, this song gave the badlands of Uttar Pradesh a sense of cool. This is 'dirty dancing' at its best and had both mass and class appeal.

Dolly Ahluwalia Tiwari, overall costume designer, is known for her attention to detail. She worked with designer Rocky S. to create the dancing costume of *'Beedi'*, a ghagra choli infused with the bling of a disco dancer. Rocky recalls: 'Bipasha has the most fabulous body, so I really wanted to focus on her midriff, so the blouse was kept short and her lehenga skirt worn low. It was bold, bright and brazen. The fuchsia and orange-sequined lehenga was teamed with a self-embroidered halter blouse. The idea was to make it look very sexy and modern, but it also needed to appeal to the masses.' Rocky kept the ghagra length to what village girls would wear, but gave the blouse a more fashionable feel by opting for a halter style. He says, 'The idea was to give it a "night clubby" feel, yet ensure it did not look out of place in the village set-up.' Finished with a large stack of bangles on both wrists, a nose stud, anklets and a tattoo-style amulet, this 'more is more' styling ensured that Bipasha sizzled in this song.

2007

Kareena Kapoor

Jab We Met

Credited Costume Designers
**Manish Malhotra (for Kareena Kapoor),
Shabina Khan (for Shahid Kapoor), Nandita Hegde,
Roopa Sood and Uma Biju (for dancers)**

An Imtiaz Ali romantic comedy that starred Kareena Kapoor and Shahid Kapoor in the lead roles, *Jab We Met* is among the 'Top 50 Romantic Bollywood Movies of All Time' according to the Internet Movie Database. Aditya Kashyap (Shahid Kapoor), a depressed and recently jilted young businessman, boards a train at Mumbai's Chhatrapati Shivaji Terminus and meets the chatterbox and hopeless romantic, Geet Dhillon (Kareena Kapoor). The train stops at a small town in the middle of the night. Lost in his sadness, Aditya decides to get down – and so does Geet, who tries to persuade him to get back on the train. Eventually they are stranded at the strange station together, and Aditya decides to help Geet find her way back to her family in Punjab's Bathinda.

It is a movie that made a huge impact on Indian fashion, thanks to its fresh take on fusion Indian dressing. Geet comes from a traditional Punjabi family, and so costume designer Manish Malhotra played with mixing Punjabi traditions with urban street style. Be it the long T-shirt worn with a Patiala, the short kurti with jeans, or the phulkari dupatta scarves, everything is injected with a little bit of bohemian *masti* (fun).

Says Manish, 'Geet is bold, she's boisterous, and she wears her Indian clothes with a day-to-day smartness.' Her casual approach to fashion is something Manish put a lot of thought into. He says, 'The whole sequence in the train is at night. So I had to think what a girl like Geet would wear at night when on a train. As Geet was a romantic, I thought of a *Mughal-e-Azam* printed T-shirt, and she wore the same salwar she wore during the day.' This is how the T-shirt worn with a salwar became a go-to for many teenage girls.

2007
Deepika Padukone

Om Shanti Om

Credited Costume Designers
Manish Malhotra, Karan Johar and Sanjeev Mulchandani

This retro-style comedy featured Deepika Padukone in her Hindi film debut; she played Shantipriya and Sandy, and Shah Rukh Khan played Om Prakash Makhija and Om Kapoor. This big-budget Farah Khan movie has a bit of everything – romance, comedy, action, drama and some fantastic song and dance numbers. It was a film whose fashion made us look back at and reflect on the golden age of Hindi cinema, especially when it came to Deepika's portrayal of Shantipriya, a leading actress from the 1970s.

Manish Malhotra, the costume designer, is known for his passion for the cinema of this period. 'Farah and I are fascinated by vintage films and 70s films. I really enjoyed doing this film because it was like going back to school and looking at these clothes', says Manish. In the song 'Dhoom Taana', there are references to Hema Malini in *Dream Girl*, Helen in *Upaasna* and even Madhuri Dixit in *Tezaab*. The tight purple kurta Deepika wears while playing badminton is inspired by the outfit in the song 'Dhal Gaya Din Ho Gayi Sham' from *Humjoli*. By changing the colour from shocking pink to purple, Manish added a fresh vibe and updated this iconic 1960s look.

Leading Indian department store chain Shopper's Stop signed a deal with the film producer to come out with a line inspired by the film – such was the interest in the retro vibe created by *Om Shanti Om*. Deepika was truly note-perfect in all her costumes.

2008
Priyanka Chopra

Dostana

Credited Costume Designers
**Aki Narula and Manish Malhotra (for Priyanka Chopra
and Shilpa Shetty)**

This Karan Johar-produced romantic comedy, directed by Tarun Mansukhani, stars John Abraham, Abhishek Bachchan and Priyanka Chopra, who play Kunal Chopra, Sameer Kapoor and Neha Melwani respectively, where both men fall in love with Neha. Based in Miami, one of America's most glamorous cities, and with Priyanka playing a fashion editor, Manish Malhotra was not scared to dial up the dazzle factor when it came to Priyanka's look.

The 'Dostana sari', as it is now known, is a contemporary take on the traditional sari. With its bikini-style blouse and thin *pallu*, its skirt was tied low so that the drape would flaunt Priyanka's perfect bikini body. For the song *'Desi Girl'*, it seems that both Karan Johar and Tarun Mansukhani wanted her to wear a dress or a gown – but Manish felt that a sari would work best for the film's most important song.

For Manish, there is nothing more sensuous than a sari. Since Priyanka had worn a gold-sequined swimsuit with side cut-outs in a previous scene, he felt there had to be a silver iridescent sari for the standout song of the film. He says, 'I told Karan that gold is going to make such an impact. How can we beat that impact with a sari? Why don't we do silver? There was a sequined petticoat, pre-stitched, and that's where the glow comes from.' He credits his knowledge of how to make a sari 'dance friendly' to one of the first actresses he worked with – Sridevi. There were a lot of fittings for this outfit to ensure that Priyanka could move with ease. The tag of being a *'desi* girl' that Priyanka now enjoys is thanks to this song in the film and how striking she looked in her outfit.

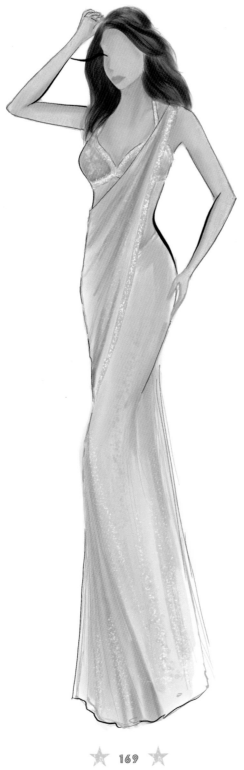

2008

Kangana Ranaut

Fashion

Credited Costume Designers
Rita Dhody (stylist)
Narendra Kumar Ahmed, Wendell Roddrigues, Shane and Falguni Peacock, Gavin Miguel, Anamika Khanna and Pam Mehta (for shows)

This was the film that put Kangana Ranaut on the fashion map. She played the supporting role of Shonali Gujral, a supermodel with a drug problem who is quickly replaced in the industry by Meghna Mathur, the film's protagonist, played by Priyanka Chopra. At the 54th annual Filmfare Awards, Priyanka Chopra won Best Actress and Kangana Ranaut bagged Best Supporting Actress for this film.

Since this was a film about fashion, costumes played a crucial role, even when the clothes seemed a bit fantastical and over the top. The costume designer for the movie was Rita Dhody, a style icon in her own right, even though she was not known for working in Bollywood. She is a fashion expert who has been on every 'best dressed' list, and was working with Harvey Nichols in Saudi Arabia as a buyer at the time. 'The film's director, Madhur Bhandarkar, was sure he needed a designer who was not from the industry but who understood fashion. And I initially rejected the project, but he pursued me for six months', says Rita. This makes sense, since fashion is obviously only the backdrop of the film. Rita adds, 'It was not a canvas for us to show off fashion or trends... the fashion had to enhance the script.'

In the song 'Mar Jaawan', where Shonali is the showstopper for fictional designer Leena Mehta, she wears a heavily embellished dress with a cut-out and a long train, styled with a red-feather cape trim. A kitsch head ornament and many bangles finish the look. Rita says, 'Just before she walks the ramp comes a scene in the green room where all the models are talking about this designer who just picks up pieces from Bangkok and adds her own elements. Which is why we styled it so over-the-top.' Though film critic Rajeev Masand says that 'on several occasions [the film] compromises authenticity for the sake of exaggerated drama', Rita points out, 'At one point in Indian fashion, everything was over-glamourized.' The styling had simply matched the film's script, and simultaneously succeeded in making the fashion world notice Kangana.

2008
Aishwarya Rai

Jodhaa Akbar

Credited Costume Designer
Neeta Lulla

The epic love story between Muslim Mughal emperor, Akbar, and Hindu Rajput princess, Jodhaa Bai, *Jodhaa Akbar* was a film that had its fair share of controversies. Many felt the script took too many liberties with history, and the movie was banned in a number of states, but that did not stop this film, directed by Ashutosh Gowariker, from being considered one of Indian cinema's most splendid costume dramas. It went on to win Best Film at the Filmfare Awards the following year.

It is not surprising that Neeta Lulla was behind the costumes – she has a knack for working well on period films as well as with Aishwarya Rai. However, it was the exquisite jewellery that received the most attention, and not just because there was so much of it. Neeta partnered with jewellery brand Tanishq and collaborated on a line that was specially made for the film and sold in their stores across India. Needless to say, many brides-to-be wanted to wear a '*Jodhaa Akbar* set' on their wedding day. 'It was one of the first brand–film collaborations', she says. Interestingly, in many cases, the jewellery was stitched onto the saris to ensure that they were not torn by the sheer weight and size of the stones.

A yellow lehenga that Jodhaa wears in the scene where she is entering the palace as Akbar's bride for the first time has become one of the most copied looks of the film. Its colour highlights the gold and uncut jewellery, so heavy that it directs your attention to the layered necklaces, *maang tika*, and the many bangles that adorn her. Neeta says that this film was one of the most challenging of her career. It took two months to research the costumes and another three months to procure the fabrics and embroideries, after which the tailoring began. The yellow lehenga was embroidered with *resham* thread, fine zari and *gota* on a base of turmeric yellow, and the contrasting green blouse helped to highlight Aishwarya's eyes. Neeta believes that there is a formula to knowing what works in a costume drama: 'It is about a relationship of understanding the director's requirements and also knowing what Aishwarya's comfort in clothing is', she says.

2008
Anushka Sharma

Rab Ne Bana Di Jodi

Credited Costume Designers
Aki Narula and Manish Malhotra (for Kajol and Rani Mukerji)

This romantic comedy directed by Aditya Chopra starred Shah Rukh Khan as the shy office clerk Surinder 'Suri' Sahni and Anushka Sharma (in her debut role) as the lively Tanni, the daughter of Suri's professor. While Suri is secretly in love with Tanni, she is not interested in him. Once engaged to a man she loved but who died in car accident on the day of their wedding, Tanni agrees to marry Suri to grant her father's dying wish. Although many were surprised at the casting of Anushka – she had some modelling experience but was not yet a known name – her spontaneity and charm soon ensured she won both the audience's and critics' praise.

While it is Suri who undergoes a makeover for a dance competition to gain his wife's affection, it is Tanni's style in this film that received a lot of attention: traditional Punjabi dressing was infused with a sense of modern style by costume designer Aki Narula. Tanni's shorter kurtis and Patialas, mainly in white or pastel colours, are highlighted by the use of phulkari accents, embroidered textiles that are part of Punjab's culture, traditionally used on head coverings such as shawls and dupattas. In *Rab Ne Bana Di Jodi*, it is used as a border on a dupatta or on a neckline and has a contemporary feel. A good example of this is in the song '*Tujh Mein Rab Dikhta Hai*', when Tanni is riding on the back of a motorbike in a white outfit with phulkari details, short silver *jhumka* earrings and stacked multi-coloured bangles. Later in the song you see her praying – and the way she goes from the motorbike to the gurdwara speaks of the life of a young, modern Indian woman.

Aki sourced Anushka's outfits from Amritsar, picking up more than 70 phulkari dupattas and using them on different outfits. Many fabric stores in North India started calling their phulkaris the '*Rab Ne Bana Di Jodi* dupatta'. Later, on India's high streets, you could see phulkari patterns used in accessories such as bags, or on Western silhouettes – on jackets and even on shirts – and the style is no doubt inspired by this film. While Anushka's look may not have been one of high fashion, its ease made it relatable.

2008
Kareena Kapoor

Tashan

Credited Costume Designer
Aki Narula

Tashan was a landmark film for Kareena Kapoor for many reasons; among them, it marked the start of her relationship with co-star Saif Ali Khan, whom she later married. It also marks the beginning of her being seen as a bonafide fashion icon. All this from a film that was panned by the critics, despite being a multi-starrer from Yash Raj Films.

In this action flick, Kareena played Pooja Singh, a woman trying to avenge her father's death. Pooja seduces call centre executive Jimmy Cliff (Saif Ali Khan), who has fallen for her and is willing to help with her plan to steal Bhaiyaji's (Anil Kapoor) money. As the story unfolds, a wannabe gangster, Bachchan Pandey (Akshay Kumar) joins their plan. As part of this cat-and-mouse chase, Kareena played a spirited and determined woman, and the costumes needed to reflect that. She wore a white bikini and also a pair of denim shorts with a crop top, complete with leather accessories and aviators. And she looked fabulous, in part thanks to the weight she lost for this role. When Kareena made her film debut in *Refugee*, she was seen as a typical Punjabi woman – fair and curvy. *Tashan* is when she became known for her size-zero figure.

It was rumoured that the actress lost 20 pounds for this role. It was from this film that the 'Kareena Kapoor diet' became the one to follow, and her dietician Rujuta Diwekar became a household name. The 'size zero' tagline that she earned for *Tashan* was first mentioned by Nishat Fatima, former editor of *Harper's Bazaar India*, while working for the *Hindustan Times*. Most importantly, costume designer Aki Narula understood how to make the most of Kareena's new, leaner figure. Nishat Fatima says, 'Kareena, possibly dressed the sexiest I've seen her, from the bikini to the crop tops, the short shorts and the boots. But who cared about what she wore? Mostly what kept your eyes on screen was just how thin she had become.'

2010s

2010
Sonam Kapoor

Aisha

Credited Costume Designers
Kunal Rawal and Pernia Qureshi

With fashionable Sonam Kapoor playing the heroine, and her equally stylish younger sister Rhea Kapoor in the role of producer, *Aisha* was a film where everyone justifiably expected the fashion to be fabulous. The script was based on Jane Austen's *Emma*, and Rajshree Ojha's directorial style reminded you of the 1995 cult teen film, and fellow *Emma* adaptation, *Clueless*. Also in the film was Ira Dubey as Aisha's best friend, Pinky Bose, and model Lisa Haydon as Aarti Menon. Both are known for their personal style, so it seems that even the casting was carried out to include 'fashion girls'.

Since Aisha is a stereotypically young, upper-middle-class, South Delhi woman, the Kapoors decided that the best person for the job of costume designer was Delhi-based fashion stylist Pernia Qureshi. Part of Delhi's style-set, she was just starting out as an independent stylist; her work on *Aisha* helped put her on the fashion map. For Aisha's wardrobe, she shopped at New York's Fifth Avenue and Delhi's Sarojini Nagar. Qureshi says, 'I wanted Aisha's character to look real. Just because she was a South Delhi, upper-class fashion enthusiast, it didn't mean she had to only wear designer clothing. The most stylish girls always have a wardrobe that has a bit of everything.' Sonam had 100-plus costume changes in the film – but there was one fashion item that received some special love, and that was the iconic Lady Dior bag. Although the bag was seen throughout the movie, the scene that instantly comes to mind is when Aisha is at a polo match, wearing a white ruffled dress, a black-bow style fascinator with a veil and the Lady Dior bag. You will notice that many of the clothes, such as the white ruffle dress, were carefully chosen to ensure the bag gained the spotlight. It spoke of how bags had become status symbols among the young, fashion-forward women of India.

Aisha's fashion was heavy on the use of designer labels, be it Anamika Khanna or Chanel. Christian Dior too worked closely with the film, and an article in *Mint* estimated that as many as 60 products from this French fashion house appeared in the film. *Aisha* seemed to make no apology for making fashion as important as its characters, and successfully established Sonam as Bollywood's ultimate fashion girl.

2010
Sonakshi Sinha

Dabangg

Credited Costume Designers
Alvira Khan Agnihotri and Ashley Rebello

This action film, directed by Abhinav Kashyap, featured Salman Khan in the lead role of a police officer, Chulbul Pandey, and also marked the debut of Sonakshi Sinha. She played a village girl, Rajjo, who hails from Uttar Pradesh and is the love interest of Chulbul. At first glance, this was not the most fashion-forward role for the actress; Sonakshi, who is a graduate of fashion design, had modelled at Lakmé Fashion Week and had worked as a costume designer in films before *Dabangg*, says, 'In a sea of skinny jeans and mini-skirts, here I was told I would be making my debut in a sari. Strangely enough, it excited me and it paid off.'

Sonakshi, who has very 'Indian' features with her almond-shaped eyes and glossy dark hair, wore lehengas and saris throughout the film. Though she had lost weight for her debut, she was still curvier than most other actresses of that time and that helped her character be more relatable. Recalls Priya Tanna, the editor of *Vogue India*, 'What people don't realize is that her clothes play a very important part in characterization and making us believe her.' However, it was the costume designers Alvira Khan Agnihotri and Ashley Rebello's use of colour that made the biggest impact. For the song 'Tere Mast Mast Do Nain', Sonakshi wore *pista* green, *haldi* yellow, rich burgundy and saffron orange. Though in the song she tended to keep blouses matching her lehenga or sari, for much of the film, the costume designers played with mismatched colours. Says Priya, 'It is not uncommon to go to smaller towns, to rural areas, and see women embracing colour. So you have a colour like yellow and then you have a blouse which is blue, which could potentially look gaudy, but in her case, it just gives [her] character a pop, a feel of spunk. In muted tones, she would have been just another village belle… prancing around her hero.'

Sonakshi's make-up was simple so that her glowing skin shone through. This, combined with the use of clever colour combinations in the clothing, added a contemporary feel to the timeless village belle look. In smaller cities in India, you can see many sari shops advertising that they sell 'the *Dabangg* look' – the fashion of this film definitely struck a chord with the heartlands of India.

2010

Aishwarya Rai

Guzaarish

Credited Costume Designers
Sabyasachi and Mohsen Nathani (background costumes)

This was the second time that designer Sabyasachi worked with filmmaker Sanjay Leela Bhansali – known for his grand storytelling, opulent sets and rich costumes – and marked a move towards a more surreal style of storytelling. Aishwarya Rai played Sofia D'Souza, a nurse who looks after Ethan Mascarenhas, a quadriplegic person, played by Hrithik Roshan. The film is set in Goa, and Bhansali stays true to the Portuguese heritage of this city.

Says Sabyasachi, 'I got a lot of criticism for the clothes for *Guzaarish*. About the fact that, for a nurse, the character was overdressed. But as a costume designer, one pays homage to the director's artistic vision, because that is the supreme viewpoint. A costume designer is merely a spare part and one cannot bring in personal ego.' In the song *'Udi'*, Sofia's long black-and-red dress has tiers and frills that seem inspired by the costume of a flamenco dancer. Her hair is braided and a rose is placed on one side. Every detail was thought out. Says Sabyasachi, 'I have a way of describing things and I called it the "gothic *choti*", and Sanjay was more in love with the name than the hairstyle itself. He insisted I do that hair for that look. There are many nuances of Frida Kahlo in the film, and for me, a braid is synonymous with her.'

The quirky jewellery that Aishwarya wore throughout the film was custom-made and represented her eclectic tastes. Even the shade of red lipstick that she wore had a meaning, and Sabyasachi says that it 'symbolized a defense mechanism, but was interpreted as wantonness by critics. Sometimes, when you are dealing with a complex character, clothing becomes a language in itself.' Hence, there was the choice of black and red colours to symbolize the self-imposed suppression of a vibrant life.

2010

Katrina Kaif

Tees Maar Khan

Credited Costume Designers
Aki Narula and Sanjiv Mulchandani

A Farah Khan film that starred Akshay Kumar, Katrina Kaif and Akshaye Khanna, this movie is an adaptation of the 1966 comedy, *After the Fox*. Tabrez Khan (Akshay Kumar) is a criminal who plans on looting a train carrying antique treasure. In order to do so, he poses as a famous Hollywood director, pretends to make a period film in a village and cons a Bollywood superstar, Aatish Kapoor (Akshaye Khanna), to star in it. Anya Khan (Katrina Kaif) is Tabrez's wannabe actress wife.

The film, which received negative reviews from most movie critics, is mostly remembered today for the song *'Sheila Ki Jawani'*. Wearing just a white satin bedsheet under pink lighting, Katrina had never looked so sensuous – it was meant to be a Bhojpuri-style song and Katrina managed to be raunchy yet graceful. Her outfit showed off her slim figure; she had revealed in interviews that she worked out for six months in order to ensure she was in perfect shape. It was worth it: she practically sizzled. Seven years later, Katrina was the first Indian film star to be part of fashion photographer Mario Testino's 'Towel Series', joining Blake Lively, Cindy Crawford and Kendall Jenner, all of whom were shot wearing nothing but towels. Those seductive pictures evoked the same, iconic body confidence that Katrina had displayed while wearing just a bed sheet for *'Sheila Ki Jawani'*.

2011
Vidya Balan

The Dirty Picture

Credited Costume Designer
Niharika Bhasin Khan

This was the film that cemented Vidya Balan as one of Indian cinema's finest actors. Her fearless portrayal of yesteryear South Indian star Silk Smitha won her Best Actress accolades across the board, from the National Awards to the Filmfare Awards. Though Vidya bears little resemblance to the ill-fated Silk, her performance was truly excellent.

The Dirty Picture also gave costume designer Niharika Bhasin Khan her first National Award for Best Costume Design. She worked on all the characters of the film, so the whole look and feel when it comes to clothes can be credited to her. Niharika says that she never grew up watching Indian movies, so there was a lot of referencing and research involved to ensure that the film's sense of fashion stayed true to Silk's. Low necklines were a must for the wardrobe, and cholis had to be short while waists were worn very low – yet they never seemed 'vulgar'. Famously, Vidya even padded herself up for certain scenes so that she looked as curvy in her clothes as the real Silk did. Custom-made costumes were therefore crafted to suit both Vidya's body and the style of the film; all these garments had to be specially commissioned, and over 135 outfits were tailored for the film.

Niharika says that one of the challenges was that 'North Indians tend to look down on South Indian cinema, but films from the South have their own charm. So we had to try to balance the North's perception with the South's style of filmmaking very carefully.' This shows in the pink dhoti teamed with a short blouse for the song '*Ooh La La*'. For this costume, Niharika used shiny pink lurex, and explains that the pearl embellishment was a deliberate choice: 'Since the fabric was so shiny, I did not want to use sequins, as that would have made it [the look] seem too much. I did want to play to stereotypes and so the pearls act as a balance, adding flamboyance without pushing the look too far.' It was this skilful approach by Niharika and her team that played a large role in making the audience believe that Vidya was indeed Silk Smitha.

2011
Nargis Fakhri

Rockstar

Credited Costume Designers
Manish Malhotra, Aki Narula and Dolly Ahluwalia Tiwari

Rockstar is a film about an ill-fated romance between Janardhan 'Jordan' Jakhar (Ranbir Kapoor), a Delhi boy who goes from being a college nerd to an international music phenomenon, and Heer Kaul (Nargis Fakhri), a beautiful Kashmiri girl, who is known at college for being a heartbreaker. Besides this film being Nargis' debut and one of Ranbir's most noteworthy performances to date, this movie invited people to look at the rich heritage of Kashmiri craft in a new light.

Director Imtiaz Ali was clear that the wedding of Heer had to look like a true Kashmiri Pandit wedding. You can see this from the details that both Imitaz and costume designer Manish Malhotra put into the wedding scene, from the *tarang* to the *dejhor* to the *jhumar*. Recalls Manish, 'The whole look was inspired by Delhi meets Kashmir.' Indeed, *tilla* and fine zari from Kashmir were given the spotlight in the costumes of this film, while Delhi's style can be seen in the heavy uncut diamond necklaces Heer wears. Her character's modest lehenga in hues of orange and red with a green border is a meeting of the Manish Malhotra aesthetic with Kashmir's craftsmanship. Even today, Manish references the fine craftsmanship of this region in his fashion collection. 'Kashmir is so beautiful, untouched, pretty and a little forgotten in terms of handicrafts, and that's why I wanted to revive that.' Though Nargis' acting abilities received much criticism, she had such poise in the wedding scene that it ensured that this was one of the film's most beautiful moments.

2011
Bagwati

Zindagi Na Milegi Dobara

Credited Costume Designer
Arjun Bhasin

By now the brother-and-sister duo, Farhan and Zoya Akhtar, had established themselves as the faces of cool when it came to Indian cinema. This was Zoya's second film, and she cast her brother as one of the leads. The film focuses on three friends, Kabir (Abhay Deol), Arjun (Hrithik Roshan) and Imraan (Farhan Akhtar), who take a road trip across Spain for Kabir's bachelor party. Kabir is all set to marry his girlfriend, Natasha Arora (Kalki Koechlin), who is an interior designer with a penchant for high fashion. Although Natasha is extremely fashion-conscious, and Arjun's love interest, Laila (Katrina Kaif), has a memorable wardrobe with a carefree feel, fashion-wise it was the orange ostrich-skin Hermès Kelly bag, 'Bagwati', that stole the film.

In the movie, Kabir is to gift the bag to his fiancée and asks Arjun to purchase it on his behalf. Natasha is the daughter of a millionaire hotelier and is very affected by society and what people think of her; naturally, she needs to have the hottest, latest and most expensive bag. This was a reflection of how fashion, and the handbag in particular, had become a status symbol in the upper strata of Indian society.

The costume designer behind this film was the Akhtars' favourite, Arjun Bhasin. He recalls that they wanted the bag, Bagwati, to have a personality of 'her' own. 'Zoya and I discussed if it should be a Dior or a Chloé. The idea was to talk about how the influx of foreign fashion labels in India had affected the higher echelons of society.' The Hermès Kelly was chosen because it seemed that there could be nothing more iconic than an Hermès bag. In addition, the Kelly in ostrich leather (which then retailed for around 12,000 euros, or approximately Rs. 9.5 lakhs) looked perfect, complete with a pair of sunglasses and a hat. With the enormous success of *Zindagi Na Milegi Dobara*, Bagwati remains one of Indian cinema's most beloved 'characters'.

2012

Deepika Padukone

Cocktail

Credited Costume Designer
Anaita Shroff Adajania

Though a forward-thinking film for a young, modern and urban audience, *Cocktail* had all the classic histrionics you would expect from an old-fashioned Bollywood romance. Based in London, the film is about a love triangle between Gautam Kapoor (Saif Ali Khan), Veronica Malaney (Deepika Padukone) and Meera Sahni (newcomer Diana Penty). The film's costume designer was Anaita Shroff Adajania, and the director was her husband, Homi Adajania. Anaita is one of India's most sought-after fashion stylists, being the fashion director of *Vogue India* and at the forefront of her own styling company, Style Cell. Homi is one of Indian cinema's cool-age directors, with movies such as *Being Cyrus* and *Finding Fanny* under his belt. Hence, the fashion in this film was, as the Instagram generation likes to call it, 'on point'.

Veronica is a stylish and spoilt rich kid who makes heads turn when she walks into a nightclub. Any fashion-savvy woman knows how to mix high and street fashion with élan, and this is what Anaita did for Deepika, making it the actress' hippest on-screen moment. Says Anaita, 'It was about her being true to her character. Veronica had a casual, sexy look that actually was inherent to the character. With *Cocktail*, the canvas allowed me to be fashion-forward. I remember needing everyone at the shooting stage to trust my sensibilities that many of the costumes would become trendy by the time the film would release a year later. It was a risk, but I was very confident that the looks would not only be a part of future trends, but that they would create future trends.'

It was the fashion that was perhaps more talked about than anything else in *Cocktail*. A high point was Deepika's Aztec skirt, which was teamed with a pair of sunglasses and a grey T-shirt that was knotted above the waist. This was prominently featured in the posters, serving as a first look into *Cocktail*, and soon everyone wanted to know where the outfit was from. The sunglasses were from Dior and the skirt was from the contemporary British label All Saints, which was not yet so well-known in India. But with that one poster, suddenly many young Indian women wanted to shop for their entire summer wardrobe at this store.

2012
Kareena Kapoor

Dabangg 2

Credited Costume Designers

Alvira Khan Agnihotri and Ashley Rebello

The second instalment in the *Dabangg* series, this film was directed by Arbaaz Khan. Salman Khan reprised his role as Inspector Chulbul Pandey, and so did Sonakshi Sinha with her role as Rajjo Pandey. Both Malaika Arora Khan and Kareena Kapoor made special appearances for item numbers, and Kareena's '*Fevicol Se*' became an instant rage. Her first on-screen appearance after her marriage to Saif Ali Khan, the song confirmed that Kareena was not letting her change in marital status affect her career. Malaika was also a producer on the film, and in an interview with the *Times of India* in 2012, Kareena thanked her for taking charge of everything, including costumes.

However, it was Manish Malhotra who was primarily responsible for Kareena's look in '*Fevicol Se*'. He says, 'Farah Khan was the choreographer and she wanted a metallic, rustic, sequined dance-girl kind of look. This was a very in-your-face blouse. But the colours that I chose were very metallic and modern to keep it contemporary.' Her short black choli with a deep cut-out back and multi-coloured pom-poms became quite a sensation. It was clearly meant to draw your attention to Kareena's perfect figure. While the skirt looked like a sari tied around the waist, it was all pre-stitched. 'I had done something like that for Kareena in *Ra.One*'s "*Chammak Challo*". It is all very fitted', adds Manish. Voluminous, bouncy hair and simple hoop earrings gave a carefree and easy feel to the look; a nose ring gave it an ethnic edge. This was a modern and alluring take on the village belle look of the 1960s.

Sridevi

English Vinglish

Credited Costume Designers
Sabyasachi (for Sridevi), Aarti Patkar, Nikita Raheja and Vera Chow

In Sridevi's comeback film, she played Shashi, a Pune-based housewife who is often mocked by her daughter and husband for her poor English skills. When she goes to New York for her niece's wedding, she secretly attends English classes. Sridevi's choice of this non-glam role to make her comeback pointed to her love of good filmmaking. In one of the film's most memorable scenes, she walks down the streets of Manhattan in a printed red and white cotton sari worn with a trench coat, with a takeaway coffee cup in her hand.

Sridevi wore saris throughout the film, and her costume designer, Sabyasachi, ensured that all sourcing was done from cottage emporiums or small sari shops to keep things authentic. He says, 'There was nothing "Sabyasachi" about the clothing, including the fitting of the blouse. All our blouses that we do for couture are hand-helmed, but this was stitched with a lock-stitch machine… stitched and finished [for] Rs. 100 in 2x2 Rubia.' Nothing was 'designer', as Sabyasachi ensured that everything Sridevi wore could be afforded by middle-class women. Even the handbags accrued were from Indian brands and fit within a 5,000-rupee price point, as that is what a woman like Shashi would deem acceptable.

The coat was a thrift-shop buy; while it might seem odd to wear a coat in the summer, Sabyasachi points out, 'When you are moving from Pune to New York, even a New York summer can become a cold winter. Our reaction to weather and our clothing is very relative to our place of origin. I think it was telling that a woman chose to wear a coat in peak summer in New York. The coat stood for many things. It stood for adjustment, for protection against vulnerability, and also for embracing a new life while keeping the core constant, which in this was symbolized by the sari.'

2012
Alia Bhatt

Student of the Year

Credited Costume Designer
Manish Malhotra

This film, directed by Karan Johar, marked the debuts of Alia Bhatt, Varun Dhawan and Sidharth Malhotra. A college-based romantic comedy, this film starts 10 years after graduation and then goes into flashback mode. Rohan Nanda (Varun Dhawan), the spoilt son of a rich businessman, is dating the fashion-loving Shanaya Singhania (Alia Bhatt). Suddenly, the handsome young Abhimanyu Singh (Sidharth Malhotra) joins and becomes the new centre of attention, sparking a love triangle. Set against this is the 'Student of the Year' competition that the college is holding.

Alia Bhatt was not Karan's first choice, according to an interview the director gave to the Press Trust of India. Multiple women had gone through the screen test, but he was looking for someone with that 'X factor', and so Alia was suggested. Although she suited the role, she was apparently curvier than Karan wanted, so he was unsure about casting her; Alia agreed to lose weight, and that is how she became Shanaya.

Playing a young woman who loved her fashion meant she had to look the part. Costume designer Manish Malhotra says, 'I remember giving her the first fitting for the first time… I came out of the room and knew she had it in her to be a style icon. I remember that a blouse was not fitting her, and she immediately had a solution to the problem. She understood clothes.'

Alia's look is very *Gossip Girl*'s Blair Waldorf meets *Clueless*'s Cher, and an Hermès Birkin and Lady Dior are among her go-to bags. Her schoolgirl look with the fitted blazer, headband and designer bag quickly became iconic. 'It was that ultimate spoilt kid look', says Manish. It established Alia as film's new fashion girl. Two years later, when Alia designed several capsule collections for shopping portal Jabong for an eponymous line of clothing, she credited her experience in this film for making her fall in love with fashion.

2013
Deepika Padukone

Chennai Express

Credited Costume Designers
Manish Malhotra, Shiraj Siddique, Mehek Navin Shetty and Jimmy

This Shah Rukh Khan and Deepika Padukone film, directed by Rohit Shetty, went on to become one of Indian cinema's highest-grossing films. In this action-comedy flick, Deepika played Meenalochni 'Meena' Azhagusundaram, the daughter of a local don who controls the mafia in Tamil Nadu. Shah Rukh played Rahul Mithaiwala, a Mumbai boy who, aboard the Chennai Express train, meets Meena, who is running away from a forced marriage.

Deepika's outfit in the movie poster instantly catches the eye because it is so unique. For the trailer and publicity shots, Deepika wore a blue Madras-checked lungi teamed with a bright shirt that was knotted below the bust. Costume designer Manish Malhotra explains, 'It was actually Shah Rukh Khan's concept and idea.' The lungi was draped to shorten it, and this infused a bit of playfulness to Deepika's look.

The aviator sunglasses Deepika wore almost became a trademark look, especially since she wore them again with a typical Bharatanatyam costume for another poster. Complete with a *gajra*, the modern sunglasses added a quirky touch, in line with the carefree personality of Meena. For the rest of the film, to keep things more authentic, Manish opted for silk Kanjeevaram saris. Colour blocking was key, which added a twist to the 'Southern belle' look.

2013
Priyanka Chopra

Goliyon Ki Raasleela Ram-Leela

Credited Costume Designers
Anju Modi and Maxima Basu

Sanjay Leela Bhansali is known for his costume dramas, and also for choosing well-known fashion designers for his films. For this tale about ill-fated lovers, he invited Delhi's Anju Modi – a designer with over 25 years of experience, but who had never worked in film before – to join the project, along with Maxima Basu (who had previously worked as an assistant director for the Hollywood film, *Slumdog Millionaire*). Anju is known for her knowledge of crafts and often travels to craft clusters in Gujarat, as she likes to work closely with her craftsmen. This was therefore the perfect film for her as it is set in Gujarat, a state whose rich textile and embroidery heritage she refers to quite often in her collections. The film paired Deepika Padukone, who played Leela, with Ranveer Singh, who played Ram, and they wore beautiful costumes that showed off the Kutch region's crafts and textiles. All the jewellery was sourced from the brand Amrapali, which gave Anju stunning pieces from their archives. She visited many museums across India to understand the aesthetic of the time, and her attention to detail received praise from both film and fashion critics.

Priyanka Chopra made a cameo appearance for an item song, playing a courtesan commenting on the primary relationship in the film, and wore something that seemed almost pared down next to Deepika's heavily embellished ensembles. But it is perhaps for this reason that Priyanka's outfit stands out in the film. For her song, *'Ram Chahe Leela'*, she wore a dhoti-style skirt, draped like a lungi to reveal her legs. With a low-cut blouse, her midriff was revealed, while the three-quarter sleeves gave the look elegance. 'She had to look very appealing, yet free spirited, so we decided to go with a white-on-white ensemble with delicate Gujarati mirror-work embroidery', says Anju. Since the music for this song also had some elements taken from Gujarati folk traditions, it was a perfect fit. The blouse was in khadi and the skirt in silk *chanderi*, and these fabrics were chosen due to their raw and organic look. That this simple white outfit is considered one of the key fashion moments of the film shows how Anju was able to capture the mood of that moment by way of costume.

2013
Kangana Ranaut

Krrish 3

Credited Costume Designers
Anaita Shroff, Manish Malhotra, Gavin Miguel, Kunal Rohira, Anirudh and Deepika Singh, and Uma (for dancers)

The *Krrish* series remains one of Hrithik Roshan's career highlights; he had a double role as Rohit Mehra and the superhero Krrish. Directed by his father, Rakesh Roshan, it is considered to be one of India's most successful science-fiction series. But for fashion, it is the third instalment that matters. Kangana Ranaut played Kaya, a mutant who may remind you of Dutch supermodel Lara Stone with her attitude and look.

The designer behind her look was Gavin Miguel, who had worked with Kangana multiple times in the past. He says, 'In fact, I remember working with her on many photo shoots, too… even on a portfolio of hers before she became an actress. I was brought into the film very last-minute by Kangana, as she knew I loved working on experimental projects.' He recalls that Rakesh Roshan was keen on Kaya being styled like Catwoman. 'I was clear that this character should have her own style, and that's why the metallic blue. And I had the fabric sourced in London and made the outfits at my studio.'

With her twirled high ponytail on one side, bouffant hair and latex, skin-tight dress, she looked like a form-changing alien. The look was completed with metallic nail tips. While the costume looked simple, it took Kangana more than three hours to get ready. She had to use special oils and powders to slip into the costume. Gavin explains, 'It was a tight schedule and I was there throughout; it was one of the most hectic and challenging projects I have worked on. A newspaper reported that each suit cost Rs.10 lakhs and in total 10 suits were made for the film – so that's around Rs. 1 crore worth of rubber outfits.' Though Gavin will not comment on the precise cost, he says, 'It was very expensive and we had to have multiple costumes in case of any rips and tears.'

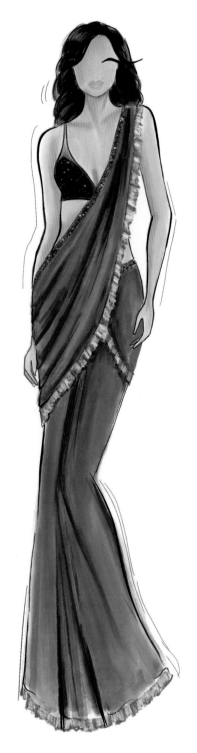

2013
Deepika Padukone

Yeh Jawaani Hai Deewani

Credited Costume Designers
**Manish Malhotra (for Ranbir Kapoor and Deepika Padukone)
and Samidha Wangnoo**

This romantic comedy directed by Ayan Mukerji featured Ranbir Kapoor and Deepika Padukone in the lead roles. Kabir 'Bunny' Thapar (Ranbir Kapoor) and Naina (Deepika Padukone), poles apart as they are, end up going on a trekking holiday to Manali with a group of friends, and from there, the story becomes one of opposites attracting. Besides being one of that year's biggest successes at the box-office, its fashion was also a commercial success. The cobalt blue georgette sari that Deepika wore in the song '*Badtameez Dil*' retailed on the e-tail site Pernia's Pop-Up Shop and was sold out within hours.

'It's a sari that I still get asked for', says the film's costume designer, Manish Malhotra. The bright colour and gold-sequined frill border teamed with a black bikini-cut blouse made it striking yet simple, and the sort of sari you can imagine yourself dancing the night away in. The sari exuded a playful and flirty vibe, and since in this scene Naina is trying to impress Bunny, it works well. Manish says, 'You will not believe it, but that sari was made in two hours. In the afternoon, we were told that they wanted it for a photo shoot that evening. For the border, we frilled a sequined fabric. I wanted to make a very cool sari for her.' Now the frill border has become a signature part of Manish's collections.

2014
Alia Bhatt

2 States

Credited Costume Designers
Manish Malhotra (for Alia Bhatt), Shiraz Siddique (for Arjun Kapoor), Natascha Charak and Nikita Mohanty (secondary costumes)

Based on Chetan Bhagat's best-selling book of the same name, *2 States* is about the love story between Ananya Swaminathan (Alia Bhatt), ranked top in her college, and Krish Malhotra (Arjun Kapoor), an MBA student. Ananya is from a typical 'Tam-Brahm' family; she wears cotton T-shirts with flared ghagra-style skirts and kurtis, and is very much an archetypal Indian college student who enjoys fusion fashion.

For the wedding scene, however, she wears a traditional Kanjeevaram sari in yellow that has a blue and pink border. The colours are vibrant and work well with the feel of the Big Fat Indian Wedding that she is attending. The movie's costume designer, Manish Malhotra, adds that the bright yellow was actually chosen by the director, Abhishek Varman. Manish also reveals some more interesting facts about the outfit: 'The sari wasn't specially woven for the film. The fabrics were sourced in Mumbai and then we cut them and completely re-sewed them. That's something I do a lot. In the earlier days, Rakhee and Rekha were also known to do this. They used to pick up 2–3 saris and cut them – so this *pallu* would go on that sari and this border on another sari. So the saris became very exclusive.' In addition, since Alia had to dance and sing in the wedding scene, the sari was pre-stitched. Adds Manish, 'It's actually fully structured.' Though the sari looked traditional, it was the structure that made the sari look so elegant while Alia danced.

The film also helped a new generation appreciate the beauty of these South Indian silk saris that originate from the small town of Kanchipuram, near Chennai. In Tamil Nadu they are a must-have in every young woman's trousseau, and are known for their vibrant colours in fine silk and use of zari in traditional motifs.

2014

Kangana Ranaut

Queen

Credited Costume Designers
Rushi Sharma and Manoshi Nath

This is the film that confirmed Kangana Ranaut's entry into Indian cinema's list of reigning leading ladies. She played a simple, young Punjabi woman, Rani, who is stood up at the altar and decides to go on her honeymoon to Europe on her own. The film follows her on this trip, and shows her transformation into a truly confident woman who learns to take control of her life, albeit with some comical hiccups. The costumes were designed by Rushi Sharma and Manoshi Nath, the duo who worked on *Oye Lucky! Lucky Oye!* and *Shanghai*, winning the Filmfare Award for Best Costume Designer for both films. Say the duo, 'When the story of *Queen* came to us, it was like listening to our own story of girlhood. Rani is each one of us – maybe not in her location or her background, but her struggle for identity and finding her own self, her first heartbreak and then her escape from her parents' cocoon. All of us have been at that threshold at some point.' At the start of the film, to reflect her small-town origins, Rani mainly wears salwar-kameezes and churidars. Her style evolves, but she manages to keep things fusion as she teams jeans with fitted kurtas and then layers them with a knit. She wears little to no make-up for most of the film and her hair is simply tied back.

The designers made most of the clothes themselves, sourcing many fabrics from Delhi's Sarojini Nagar. They credit Kangana's confidence to making the whole look and feel of this film come alive: 'Once we knew that she would support our portrayal of Rani to the fullest – the de-glam, the anti-fit, the dowdiness, the transition of colours in costumes – our job became a dream. Kangana has a beautiful body and is very elegant. This turned out to be our biggest challenge, as we had to hide her curves in the ill-fitting kurtis. Her jeans had to fall loose on the hips or thighs and yet have a bell bottom. Or they had to be a capri-length with appliqué flowers.' They further add that the knitted cardigan 'is [the character's] protective shield and her identity, which, during the "*Hungama*" song, she rips off, twirls in the air and then… calmly stuffs back into her bag. Not quite ready to peel off all that's familiar to her.' However, she still has the feistiness to stop a mugger in Paris stealing from her; her mix-and-match look therefore represented the many sides of this seemingly simple young woman. This is truly well-planned costume designing.

2015

Deepika Padukone

Bajirao Mastani

Credited Costume Designers
Anju Modi and Maxima Basu (supporting cast)

A true magnum opus from Sanjay Leela Bhansali, this film's script was based on the romance between an eighteenth-century Maratha king, Bajirao (Ranveer Singh), and Mastani (Deepika Padukone), his half-Persian second wife. The film is full of beautiful fashion, all based on exquisite tradition and craft. For the second time, Bhansali chose to work with Anju Modi for many of the costumes in the film. She is known for her knowledge of textiles and embroidery, and this shows in the outfit worn by Deepika Padukone as she dances in the song 'Deewani Mastani'. She wears a dhani-coloured kalidaar anarkali over a multi-panelled ghagra with a pair of ijhaars and looks nothing short of ethereal while she is dancing. There is such lightness in the outfit – it is a moment of sheer beauty. Although Peshwa women historically wore heavier fabrics, the designer opted for diaphanous material to give the outfit a graceful look and also make it more film-friendly. It was embroidered with gota patti as opposed to heavier embellishments to reduce the weight of the garment. Indeed, at the beginning of the film, a disclaimer makes it clear that liberties were taken with settings and costumes.

During her research, Anju found a miniature portrait of Mastani wearing a Persian hat, and in keeping with this, the jewellery was kept Persian, which is why the hand ornaments were made without using precious stones, and just with flat, antiquated gold. Mastani's father was a Rajput, but Anju decided to keep drawing upon her mother's Persian heritage for the song. She says, '"Deewani Mastani" was Mastani's first appearance at the Maratha durbar and it was only apt if we gave them a surprise element, a Persian beauty they had never seen before.' You also cannot help but feel that the song was an ode to Mughal-e-Azam's 'Pyaar Kiya To Darna Kya'. Says Anju, 'Mughal-e-Azam was a huge inspiration for Sanjay Leela Bhansali; therefore a few references were taken from the movie.' Anju won numerous awards for her work in this film, including Filmfare's Best Costume Designer, which she shared with Maxima Basu. Interestingly, Deepika later walked the catwalk at Anju's fashion show in Delhi, which took place just before the film's release. Although Deepika was a showstopper, it was difficult to top the moment from Bajirao Mastani where she looked like she had walked right out of Mastani's portrait picture.

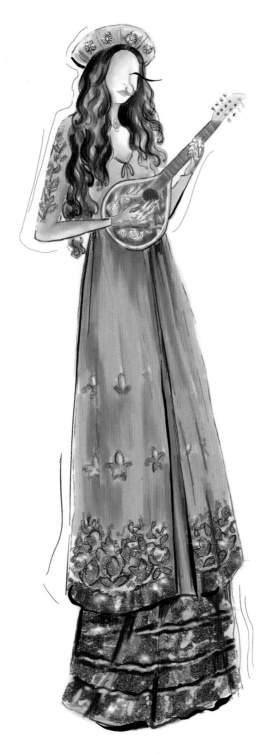

2015
Raveena Tandon

Bombay Velvet

Credited Costume Designer
Niharika Bhasin Khan

This Anurag Kashyap film is based on the relationship between the worlds of crime and business of the 1960s in India's commercial capital, Bombay. The lead roles feature Anushka Sharma as the jazz singer, Rosie, and Ranbir Kapoor as the boxer, Balraj, who falls in love with her and then makes it his life's ambition to become a 'big shot' to woo her. It is a visual delight with its vintage sets and sumptuous costumes. The film had a retro gangster approach to its look and required Outré fashion. Crucially, Raveena Tandon made a 'friendly appearance' after a long hiatus from mainstream cinema, and her cameo reminds us why, at the peak of her career in the 1990s, she was known as 'Ravishing Ravs'.

The costume designer, Niharika Bhasin Khan, says this film is one of the highlights of her career. She won a Stardust Award for Best Costume Designer because the film's outfits were so full of detail – though the one that everyone remembers is the peacock dress worn by Raveena. Since both Anushka and Raveena played jazz singers, Niharika ensured both had visibly distinct styles. As Anushka played a younger woman who moved from Goa to the big city, her clothes were kept glamorous but not over the top.

On the other hand, Raveena's character had natural flamboyance, so for the song *Mohabbat Buri Bimari*', she wore a peacock dress by Mumbai-based designer Swapnil Shinde, complete with couture-esque headgear. It was a vibrant purple with keyhole details, and the feathers were collected by Niharika from a trek in Nainital just before the shoot. She says, 'I had never seen such a range of feathers – so oversized.' The plumes for the headpiece and the trail of the dress were hand-sewn by Niharika's team the night before the shoot. Niharika says, 'I cried at the shoot, as they put a blue light on my dress, and that washed out the details.' Eventually she persuaded Kashyap to do a back shot, and that frame is the one that will always be associated with the decadence this film stood to portray. 'Raveena just oozes sensuality, and she made this dress come alive', says Niharika. The whole crew gave Niharika a standing ovation once they finished the shoot, as she had managed to deliver something that was both original and fantastical.

2018

Deepika Padukone

Padmaavat

Credited Costume Designers
Rimple and Harpreet Narula, Chandrakant Sonawane, Ajay Kmr (background) and Maxima Basu (supporting cast)

This is an epic period drama directed by Sanjay Leela Bhansali, with Deepika Padukone playing the lead, Queen Padmavati. Set in medieval Rajasthan, the cinematic focus is on Padmavati, the wife of a noble king, played by Shahid Kapoor. Such is her beauty that Emperor Alauddin Khilji, portrayed by Ranveer Singh, decides to pursue her at any cost. This story was recounted by sixteenth-century Sufi poet Malik Muhammad Jayasi, and whether it is based on fact or fiction is still a matter of debate.

The film involved some truly decadent designs when it came to costumes – Bhansali picked Delhi's hitherto little-known couturiers Rimple and Harpreet Narula as the costume designers for his masterpiece. Their brand, known for its opulent bridal couture, had just designed two collections based on this era, so they were almost a perfect fit for the film's aesthetic. They designed the clothes for all three leads, but it was Deepika's ensembles (particularly the ghagra she wore for the song 'Ghoomar'), full of regal magnificence, that mesmerized audiences.

The outfit that Deepika wore in 'Ghoomar' weighs well over 15 kilograms; it took 8,000 hours and the work of 24 skilled craftsmen to create the epic ensemble. Bright, organic cotton fabric was ornamented with lightweight zari and kachi-patti embroidery. Despite multiple tests, Deepika apparently never complained about the weight of the outfit and danced with ease at all times.

The designers say, 'The brief we got from Mr. Bhansali for the "Ghoomar" sequence ghagra and odhna that Deepika dons was that the outfit should be an embodiment of the character's metamorphosis from Sinhalese princess to the new queen of Chittor. We did intensive research on how the royal costumes might have looked, keeping both the period and province in focus, as there is much ambiguity about the same.' With layers of jewellery designed by Tanishq and many of the motifs used on the lehenga inspired from old pichwai fabrics, this outfit is truly museum-worthy. The leheriya print on the odhna was, in fact, referenced from a sixteenth-century textile sample the designers saw at the Victoria and Albert Museum in London.

2018
Veere Di Wedding

Kareena Kapoor, Sonam Kapoor, Swara Bhaskar and Shikha Talsania

Credited Costume Designers
Abu Jani–Sandeep Khosla and Rhea Kapoor

Veere Di Wedding stars four women who play best friends, or *veeres* (brothers), as they call themselves. It centres on the upcoming marriage of Kalindi, played by Kareena Kapoor, whose friends include Avni, a lawyer, portrayed by Sonam Kapoor; Sakshi, the moneyed brat, played by Swara Bhaskar; and Meera, depicted by Shikha Talsania, who is married to a doting American husband. The film was polarizing – it was banned in Kuwait and Pakistan as it was considered too sexually explicit, and received mixed reviews from audiences. But whatever people thought of the film, its fashion was so talked about that it had a definite impact.

Shashanka Ghosh, the director, used fashion to communicate personality when he directed *Veere Di Wedding*; the film's producer, Rhea Kapoor, worked closely with Abu Jani and Sandeep Khosla to secure this vision. Kareena carries off Kalindi's take on street fashion like a true clotheshorse. Avni dresses prissily, except for the night she hopes to hook up with a prospective groom, and then she wears a bikini-style blouse with a lehenga. Then there is the brazen Sakshi in her Calvin Klein bra-tops with shirts worn open. Meera dresses up her healthier physique as fashionably as the rest – with Shikha being an advocate for size equality, *Veere Di Wedding* sparked conversations around diversity within Indian fashion.

In the song '*Bhangra Ta Sajda*', the four women are dressed in classic Abu–Sandeep ensembles, with mirror work on their clothes and the use of vibrant multi-colours. In fact, the digitally-printed miniatures on Sonam's blouse were taken from a collection the designers created almost 30 years ago. While Sonam wears a white-based blouse with her skirt, Kareena, who is the bride, has fun *shibori* sleeves and a *maang tika*. The rich rebel, Swara, wears a 10-panel ghagra, a silk and *gota* skirt that has a thigh-high slit, with a denim jacket; Shikha is dressed in a flattering anarkali.

Veere Di Wedding helped give a new 'millennial cool' tag to one of India's first and most pioneering fashion labels, Abu Jani–Sandeep Khosla. This clever collaboration with film from one of India's most established design houses shows that the big screen can amplify fashion, truly making it larger than life when used intelligently.

ACKNOWLEDGEMENTS

APARNA RAM

I never thought that this day would come and that I would have the honour of thanking you all. On 15 March 2017, I met Kapil Kapoor at the London Book Fair. I presented him with an A5-sized spiral notebook that I had cobbled together at the local printers. It contained a handful of my illustrations and some text. And so, I must start with thanking Kapil and giving him credit for seeing the potential in those initial sketches. I extend my gratitude to his business partner – Priya Kapoor. Thank you so very much, Priya, for all of your wisdom and guidance, and for the endless patience you have shown through long email chains and phone calls. Corralling together a creative team based in Delhi, Dubai and London is no mean feat! Of course, this book would not be possible without its talented author – Sujata Assomull. Your eye for beauty, art and fashion, combined with your knowledge and curiosity, makes you a rare human being and a pleasure to work with. My appreciation also goes to your assistant, Hanadi, for her help in research and writing. Helping us to overcome the challenges of being in three different time zones and keeping us on track was the ever-persevering Saachi from the editorial team. Thank you, Saachi, for being a star. I'm also beholden to all the actors and designers who took time out of their busy schedules to contribute to this book. It would be far less colourful without your views and anecdotes.

I have been fortunate to have a surfeit of support from dear friends over the years. I remain eternally thankful to Ozge, a stickler for the rules of English grammar, for taking my initial scribblings and turning them into prose that I could realistically approach publishers with. Thank you, Jaspreet, for lending me your prized Bollywood books for research and for suggesting iconic costumes that I 'simply must include'. Thank you to my boys, Nav and Mos, for always giving it to me straight: 'If you don't believe in this, no one else will.' In some ways you have been key to seeing this project through to the finish line. I'm appreciative to Chris for encouraging me through every batch of illustrations, keeping me accountable and for enthusing over every single drawing. To the dynamic husband-and-wife duo – Bincy and Diana – I cannot ever hope to keep up with your energy, but thank you for supporting me, forcing me to step away from my desk and getting me out of the house!

Liz, Donna, Tricia, Debbie, Genna and Hayley – all of you have encouraged this book from when it was a mere seedling of an idea, and buoyed it through many a rejection letter, telling this Potterhead that 'J.K. Rowling was rejected loads of times before Harry Potter was published.' Thank you for never losing faith. Thank you also to my sister from another mister – Sumi. You and Shabana have always encouraged my creativity, seeing my ability more clearly than I ever did.

To my biggest frenemy, Sandy: even 8,000 miles isn't enough to keep you away. Thank you for taking (far too much!) delight in the opportunity to critique my work. 'Hell yea I'd love to insult you' has actually helped make my work better and I could never thank you enough for your support. I'm also eternally grateful to Sam – another person whom I turned to for critiquing, and who did an outstanding job.

Of course, the longest supporters of my work and talent have been my family and extended family. Sathya Uncle, you've been a published author to look up to and have paved the way for all of us rebels. Thank you, Jayabose Mama, for looking over a folder of my initial sketches so encouragingly. My dear Perima and Peripa (aunt and uncle), a gallery wall of my work in your home is truly an honour. Your love and support could never be repaid. Thank you, Ashu, for keeping me young and spreading my work to all of your friends on Instagram. My brother and sister-in-law are akin to my financial backers, buying me expensive art supplies as birthday gifts. I have appreciated every watercolour tube, and the art desk lamp that has helped me paint late into the night. Thank you!

Finally, and most importantly, thank you to Appa and Amma (Dad and Mum). Words simply aren't enough to express my gratitude. This book or any of my other work would not be possible without you both. Thank you for indulging my love for Bollywood movies and music, driving me to Wembley to buy music tapes, playing vintage Hindi songs in the car, driving me to art lessons as a teenager, proudly framing and displaying my work all over the house, and for everything else that you both do for me every single day.

SUJATA ASSOMULL

The first thank you has to go to Priya Kapoor of Roli, who thought of me for this project. It was her enthusiasm about doing a book on mainstream Indian cinema with fashion as its theme and by using illustrations that got me excited about it. Writing a book based on Indian cinematic fashion from Dubai was a bit daunting and it was the encouragement of my Indian 'media family' that kept me going, namely (in no order) Udita Jhunjunwala, Priya Tanna, Rajeev Masand, Nonita Kalra and Shefalee Vasudev. And in Dubai, I have to give a very special thanks to Hanadi Merchant Habib, who assisted with research and watched many of the films with me. She was a great sounding board, one without whom I doubt I would have been able to complete this book. Finally, I would like to thank Manish Malhotra, who took time out to write the foreword of this book and speak to me at length about his experiences in the industry; Anaita Adajania and Neeta Lulla, who always so graciously answered my many questions on fashion in films; and Rahul Mishra and Nachiket Barve who gave me insights on embroidery and textile techniques.

GLOSSARY

Alta: A red dye used to decorate hands and feet

Apsara: (Hindu mythology) A celestial nymph, typically the wife of a heavenly musician

Chanderi: A light, lustrous fabric traditionally using silk or cotton woven with metallic threads

Choli: A short-sleeved bodice or blouse worn under a sari by Indian women

Dejhor: The pendant earrings that are put on a Kashmiri Pandit bride the day before the wedding

Dhani: The light-green colour of rice inside husks

Dhoti: A garment consisting of a piece of material tied around the waist and extending to cover most of the legs

Dupatta: A length of material arranged in two folds over the chest and thrown back around the shoulders, typically worn with a salwar kameez

Gajra: A flower garland that women wear on festive occasions

Ghagra: A long full skirt, often decorated with embroidery, mirrors or bells

Gher: The girth/circumference of a lehenga

Ghungroos: The small metallic bells tied around the ankles of classical Indian dancers

Gota: An embroidery that originated in Rajasthan, often employing gold or silver ribbon

Gota patti: A traditional Indian appliqué embroidery normally using metallic-coloured ribbons

Hath-phool: A traditional Indian hand accessory that has five rings, often joined by chain-like links to a bangle or bracelet

Ikat: Fabric made using a decorative technique in which warp or weft threads, or both, are tie-dyed before weaving

Item girl: The cameo performer in a special song that does not tie into the narrative of the film but adds eye-candy and entertainment value

Jadau: A technique used in precious jewellery-making; also a term for the jewellery itself

Jhumar: An ornament that is placed in the hair and hangs over the forehead

Kachi-patti: A delicate Indian embroidery

Kalidaar: A type of panelled kurta that is similar to a frock

Khadi: Cloth hand-spun on a chakra wheel; it can be made of cotton, silk or wool

Kolhapuri: Leather slippers that originated from Kolhapur in Maharashtra

Kundan: One of the oldest forms of jewellery worn and made in India, usually containing gold and gems

Kurti: A short kurta worn by South Asian women

Leheriya: A tie-dye technique that originated in Rajasthan

Lungi: A garment similar to a sarong, wrapped around the waist and extending to the ankles

Maang tika: An ornament, usually worn in the mid-parting of a woman's hair

Mahurat: An auspicious time for an enterprise to begin or for a ceremony to take place; or an inauguration ceremony, especially one held to mark the start of the making of a film

Odhna: A type of drape, similar to a dupatta, often used as a veil

Pallu: The end of a draped sari that hangs loose

Parandi: A woman's accessory, consisting of woollen strands that are woven into the hair

Parijat: Night-flowing jasmine

Passa: A Mughal jewelled ornament worn on the side of the head, usually by brides

Patiala: Trousers for women that have their origins in Patiala, Punjab

Payal: This is the traditional Indian take on the anklet; what makes the payal special is that it has small bells that make a jingling sound

Phulkari: An ornamental cloth or shawl embroidered with silk flowers, or the style of embroidery used on a phulkari

Pichwai: Paintings on paper or cloth that generally portray Lord Krishna

Resham: A silk thread often used for intricate embroidery

Rishta: A marriage proposal

Sangeet: A celebration held before a Hindu wedding ceremony for the bride-to-be and her female friends and relatives

Sharara: A pair of loose, flared trousers worn by women, typically with a kameez and dupatta

Tarang: Traditional headgear typically worn by Kashmiri brides on their wedding day

Tilla: A Kashmiri style of embroidery that uses gold or silver thread

Zari: A type of metallic thread used decoratively on Indian clothing